Grammar
Mate 3

저자 약력

이강희 (전) 한국 외국어대학교 외국어연수 평가원 영어 전임 강사
하와이 주립대 Second Language Studies 석사
한국 외국어대학교 영어과 학사
〈Grammar's Cool〉 (YBM), 〈빠르게 잡는 유형독해 Level 2〉 (천재교육)
〈New TOEIC 콩나물 Basic Listening〉 (두산동아), 〈TOEIC CLINIC Beginner〉 (위트앤위즈덤) 등 다수의 교재 공저

전지원 미국 오리건 주립대 Linguistics 석사
(현) 한국 외국어대학교 외국어연수 평가원 영어 전임 강사
〈내공 중학 영작문〉 (다락원), 〈Grammar plus Writing〉 (다락원), 〈Grammar plus Writing Start〉 (다락원),
〈Grammar's Cool〉 (YBM), 〈빠르게 잡는 영문법〉 (천재교육) 등 다수의 교재 공저

박혜영 미국 하와이 주립대 Second Language Studies 석사
(현) 한국 외국어대학교 외국어연수 평가원 영어 전임 강사
〈내공 중학 영작문〉 (다락원), 〈Grammar plus Writing〉 (다락원), 〈Grammar plus Writing Start〉 (다락원),
〈Grammar's Cool〉 (YBM), 〈빠르게 잡는 영문법〉 (천재교육) 등 다수의 교재 공저

Grammar **Mate** ③

지은이 이강희, 전지원, 박혜영

펴낸이 정규도
펴낸곳 (주)다락원

초판 1쇄 발행 2020년 2월 10일
초판 4쇄 발행 2024년 5월 31일

편집 서정아, 서민정, 김민아
디자인 구수정
삽화 오영임
영문 감수 Michael A. Putlack

다락원 경기도 파주시 문발로 211
내용문의 (02)736-2031 내선 503
구입문의 (02)736-2031 내선 250~252

Fax (02)732-2037
출판등록 1977년 9월 16일 제406-2008-000007호

ISBN 978-89-277-0874-2 64740
         978-89-277-0871-1 64740(set)

http://www.darakwon.co.kr
다락원 홈페이지를 방문하시면 상세한 출판정보와 함께
동영상강좌, MP3 자료 등 다양한 어학 정보를 얻으실 수 있습니다.

Grammar Mate 3

DARAKWON

Introduction

Grammar Mate 시리즈는

Core basic English grammar

초급 학습자들에게 꼭 필요한 핵심 문법 사항을 수록하여 영문법의 기초를
탄탄히 다질 수 있도록 하였습니다.

Easy, clear explanations of grammar rules and concepts

문법 개념과 용어를 쉽고 명료하게 설명하였습니다. 포괄적인 문법 설명을 지양하고
세분화된 단원 구성과 포인트 별 핵심 설명으로 확실한 이해를 도울 수 있도록 하였습니다.

Plenty of various step–by-step exercises

다양하고 풍부한 연습 문제를 제공합니다. 지나친 drill이나 서술형 등 한쪽으로
치우친 유형이 아닌, 개념 이해부터 적용까지 체계적이고 다양한 문제 풀이를 통해
자연스럽게 문법 개념을 익힐 수 있습니다.

Writing exercises to develop writing skills and grammar accuracy

문법 학습 후 문장 쓰기 연습을 통해 내신 서술형에 대비할 수 있습니다.
또한 영어 문장을 써봄으로써 답을 맞추기 위한 문법이 아니라 영어라는 큰 틀 안에서
문법을 정확히 활용할 수 있도록 하였습니다.

Comprehensive tests to prepare for actual school tests

각 CHAPTER가 끝날 때마다 실제 학교 내신 시험에서 출제되는 문제 유형들로 구성된
테스트를 제공하여 학교 내신 시험에 익숙해질 수 있도록 하였습니다.

Workbook for further practice

워크북을 통한 추가 문제를 제공함으로써 문법 개념을 숙지할 때까지
충분한 문제와 복습 컨텐츠를 제공합니다.

How to Use This Book

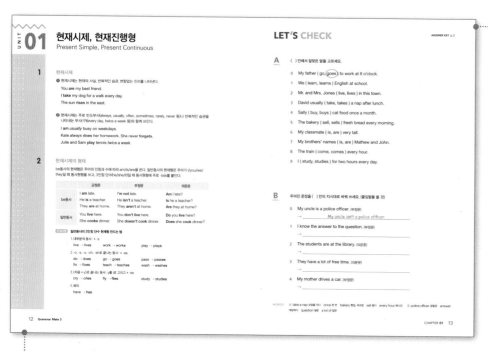

LET'S CHECK

LET'S CHECK

왼쪽 페이지에서 학습한
내용을 개념 확인 문제를
통해 바로 연습해볼 수 있
습니다.

GRAMMAR POINT

초급자가 알아야 할 문법 사항을 도표, 사진, 실용적인 예문을 통해 이해하기 쉽게 설명하였습니다.
주의해야 할 사항은 ✎NOTE 로, 더 알아야 할 사항은 +PLUS 로 제시하였습니다.

LET'S PRACTICE

보다 풍부한 연습 문제를 통해
문법 실력을 다질 수 있습니다.

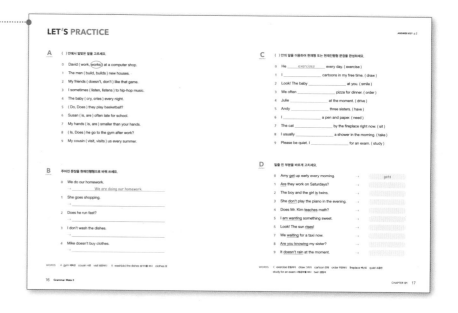

LET'S WRITE

문법 사항을 문장 쓰기에
적용해봄으로써 학습 효과를
증대시키고 내신 서술형에
대비할 수 있습니다.
빈칸 완성, 어구 배열, 영작하기
문제로 구성되어 있습니다.

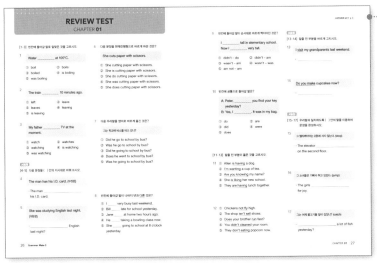

REVIEW TEST

각 CHAPTER가 끝날 때마다
학습한 문법 사항을 총 정리할
수 있고, 나아가 실제 내신 문제
유형에 익숙해질 수 있습니다.

WORKBOOK

워크북을 통해 학습한 해당
UNIT의 문법 사항을 다시 한번
복습하며 실력을 점검해볼 수
있습니다.

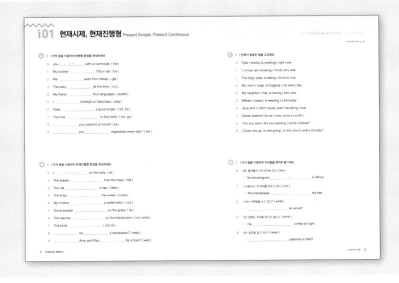

Contents

CHAPTER
01

Present &
Past Tenses
현재시제와 과거시제

LET'S LOOK

I usually **walk** to school.
Today, I **am riding** my bike to school.

I **went** to bed at 10:00 yesterday.
I **was sleeping** at 10:30.

시제는 동사의 형태를 변화시켜 어떤 일이 언제 일어났는지를 나타내주는 것이다.
현재시제는 현재의 사실, 반복적인 습관, 변함없는 진리를 나타낸다. **과거시제**는 과거
에 이미 끝난 일을 나타낸다. **진행시제**는 특정 시점에 진행 중인 일을 나타낸다.

01 현재시제, 현재진행형
Present Simple, Present Continuous

1 현재시제

❶ 현재시제는 현재의 사실, 반복적인 습관, 변함없는 진리를 나타낸다.

You **are** my best friend.

I **take** my dog for a walk every day.

The sun **rises** in the east.

❷ 현재시제는 주로 빈도부사(always, usually, often, sometimes, rarely, never 등)나 반복적인 습관을 나타내는 부사(구)(every day, twice a week 등)와 함께 쓰인다.

I **am** *usually* busy on weekdays.

Kate *always* **does** her homework. She *never* **forgets**.

Julie and Sam **play** tennis *twice a week*.

2 현재시제의 형태

be동사의 현재형은 주어의 인칭과 수에 따라 am/is/are를 쓴다. 일반동사의 현재형은 주어가 I/you/we/they일 때 동사원형을 쓰고, 3인칭 단수(he/she/it)일 때 동사원형에 주로 -(e)s를 붙인다.

	긍정문	부정문	의문문
be동사	I **am** late. He **is** a teacher. They **are** at home.	I'**m not** late. He **isn't** a teacher. They **aren't** at home.	**Am** I late? **Is** he a teacher? **Are** they at home?
일반동사	You **live** here. She **cooks** dinner.	You **don't live** here. She **doesn't cook** dinner.	**Do** you **live** here? **Does** she **cook** dinner?

✏NOTE **일반동사의 3인칭 단수 현재형 만드는 법**

1. 대부분의 동사: + -s

    live → live**s**   work → work**s**   play → play**s**

2. -o, -s, -x, -ch, -sh로 끝나는 동사: + -es

    do → do**es**   go → go**es**   pass → pass**es**

    fix → fix**es**   teach → teach**es**   wash → wash**es**

3. 〈자음 + y〉로 끝나는 동사: y를 i로 고치고 + -es

    cry → cr**ies**   fly → fl**ies**   study → stud**ies**

4. 예외

    have → **has**

LET'S CHECK

A ( ) 안에서 알맞은 말을 고르세요.

0   My father (go, (goes)) to work at 8 o'clock.

1   We (learn, learns) English at school.

2   Mr. and Mrs. Jones (live, lives) in this town.

3   David usually (take, takes) a nap after lunch.

4   Sally (buy, buys) cat food once a month.

5   The bakery (sell, sells) fresh bread every morning.

6   My classmate (is, are) very tall.

7   My brothers' names (is, are) Mathew and John.

8   The train (come, comes) every hour.

9   I (study, studies) for two hours every day.

B 주어진 문장을 ( ) 안의 지시대로 바꿔 쓰세요. (줄임말을 쓸 것)

0   My uncle is a police officer. (부정문)
→ _____My uncle isn't a police officer._____

1   I know the answer to the question. (부정문)
→ _____

2   The students are at the library. (의문문)
→ _____

3   They have a lot of free time. (의문문)
→ _____

4   My mother drives a car. (부정문)
→ _____

WORDS   A take a nap 낮잠을 자다   once 한 번   bakery 빵집, 제과점   sell 팔다   every hour 매시간   B police officer 경찰관
answer 대답, 대답하다   question 질문   a lot of 많은

3   현재진행형

❶ 현재진행형은 '~하고 있다, ~하는 중이다'의 의미로 지금 진행 중인 일을 나타낸다.

I **wash** my hair every day.

I **am washing** my hair *right now*.

❷ 현재진행형은 주로 now(지금), right now(바로 지금), at the moment(지금은) 등의 시간 표현과 함께 쓰인다.

They **are jogging** *now*.

Dad **is sleeping** *at the moment*.

4   현재진행형의 형태

❶ 현재진행형은 주어의 인칭과 수에 따라 「be동사의 현재형 + 동사원형-ing」 형태로 쓴다.

긍정문	부정문	의문문
I **am reading**.	**I'm not reading**.	**Am** I **reading**?
He **is working**.	He **isn't working**.	**Is** he **working**?
They **are studying**.	They **aren't studying**.	**Are** they **studying**?

> **✎ NOTE** 동사의 -ing형 만드는 법
>
> 1. 대부분의 동사: + -ing
>
>   go → go**ing**   rain → rain**ing**   play → play**ing**
>
> 2. -e로 끝나는 동사: e를 빼고 + -ing
>
>   come → com**ing**   make → mak**ing**   write → writ**ing**
>
> 3. 〈단모음 + 단자음〉으로 끝나는 동사: 자음을 한번 더 쓰고 + -ing
>
>   cut → cut**ting**   run → run**ning**   swim → swim**ming**
>
> 4. -ie로 끝나는 동사: ie를 y로 고치고 + -ing
>
>   die → dy**ing**   lie → ly**ing**   tie → ty**ing**

❷ 감정, 소유, 생각 등 상태를 나타내는 동사는 현재진행형을 쓰지 않고 현재시제로 쓴다.

love	want	have	know	remember
like	need	own	believe	forget

I **like** the new Italian restaurant.

My neighbor **has** a big dog.

❸ 단, have가 소유(가지다)의 뜻이 아닌 경우에는 진행형을 쓸 수 있다.

I **am having** lunch. 나는 점심 식사를 하고 있다.

We **are having** a good time. 우리는 즐거운 시간을 보내고 있다.

LET'S CHECK

C 그림을 보고 보기에서 알맞은 말을 골라 현재진행형 문장을 완성하세요. (단, 한 번씩만 쓸 것)

보기   ~~bark~~   lie   fly   run   paint   make

0 The dog ___is barking___ .

1 The man _____ the wall.

2 She _____ sandwiches.

3 He _____ in the park.

4 They _____ on the beach.

5 Two birds _____ .

D ( ) 안의 말을 이용하여 현재진행형 부정문과 의문문을 완성하세요. (줄임말을 쓸 것)

0 We ___aren't going___ to the museum. (not, go)

1 The girls _____ English. (not, speak)

2 The bus _____ . (not, move)

3 My brother _____ his homework. (not, do)

4 _____ I _____ too loudly? (sing)

5 _____ you _____ your seatbelt? (wear)

6 _____ he _____ home now? (come)

7 _____ the children _____ in the garden? (play)

WORDS   C bark 짖다   lie 눕다   D move 움직이다   loudly 큰 소리로, 시끄럽게   seatbelt 안전벨트

LET'S PRACTICE

A ( ) 안에서 알맞은 말을 고르세요.

0 David (work, (works)) at a computer shop.

1 The men (build, builds) new houses.

2 My friends (doesn't, don't) like that game.

3 I sometimes (listen, listens) to hip-hop music.

4 The baby (cry, cries) every night.

5 (Do, Does) they play basketball?

6 Susan (is, are) often late for school.

7 My hands (is, are) smaller than your hands.

8 (Is, Does) he go to the gym after work?

9 My cousin (visit, visits) us every summer.

B 주어진 문장을 현재진행형으로 바꿔 쓰세요.

0 We do our homework.
   → _____We are doing our homework._____ .

1 She goes shopping.
   → _____

2 Does he run fast?
   → _____

3 I don't wash the dishes.
   → _____

4 Mike doesn't buy clothes.
   → _____

WORDS   A build 짓다 gym 체육관 cousin 사촌 visit 방문하다   B wash[do] the dishes 설거지를 하다 clothes 옷

C ( ) 안의 말을 이용하여 현재형 또는 현재진행형 문장을 완성하세요.

0 He _____exercises_____ every day. (exercise)

1 I _____ cartoons in my free time. (draw)

2 Look! The baby _____ at you. (smile)

3 We often _____ pizza for dinner. (order)

4 Julie _____ at the moment. (drive)

5 Andy _____ three sisters. (have)

6 I _____ a pen and paper. (need)

7 The cat _____ by the fireplace right now. (sit)

8 I usually _____ a shower in the morning. (take)

9 Please be quiet. I _____ for an exam. (study)

D 밑줄 친 부분을 바르게 고치세요.

0 Amy get up early every morning.   →   gets

1 Are they work on Saturdays?   →

2 The boy and the girl is twins.   →

3 She don't play the piano in the evening. →

4 Does Mr. Kim teaches math?   →

5 I am wanting something sweet.   →

6 Look! The sun rises!   →

7 We waiting for a taxi now.   →

8 Are you knowing my sister?   →

9 It doesn't rain at the moment.   →

WORDS C exercise 운동하다 draw 그리다 cartoon 만화 order 주문하다 fireplace 벽난로 quiet 조용한
study for an exam 시험공부를 하다 twin 쌍둥이

UNIT 02 과거시제, 과거진행형
Past Simple, Past Continuous

1 과거시제

❶ 과거시제는 '〜이었다, 〜했다'의 의미로 과거에 이미 끝난 일, 역사적인 사실 등을 나타낸다.

My grandfather **was** a soldier.

I **visited** Singapore last year.

The Korean War **started** on June 25, 1950.

❷ 과거시제는 주로 yesterday(어제), last 〜(지난 〜), 〜 ago(〜 전에), in 1999(1999년에), then(그때) 등 과거를 나타내는 시간 표현과 함께 쓰인다.

My cat **was** sick *yesterday*.

I **bought** a new bag *last week*.

David first **met** his wife *five years ago*.

2 과거시제의 형태

be동사의 과거형은 was/were를 쓴다. 일반동사의 과거형은 주어의 인칭과 수에 관계없이 동사원형에 주로 -(e)d를 붙인다.

	긍정문	부정문	의문문
be동사	I **was** late. He **was** a teacher. They **were** at home.	I **wasn't** late. He **wasn't** a teacher. They **weren't** at home.	**Was** I late? **Was** he a teacher? **Were** they at home?
일반동사	You **lived** here. She **cooked** dinner.	You **didn't live** here. She **didn't cook** dinner.	**Did** you **live** here? **Did** she **cook** dinner?

✎ NOTE **일반동사의 과거형 만드는 법**

1. 대부분의 동사: + -ed

   walk → walked   help → helped   play → played

2. -e로 끝나는 동사: + -d

   love → loved   close → closed   dance → danced

3. 〈자음 + y〉로 끝나는 동사: y를 i로 고치고 + -ed

   cry → cried   try → tried   study → studied

4. 〈단모음 + 단자음〉으로 끝나는 동사: 마지막 자음을 한번 더 쓰고 + -ed

   hug → hugged   plan → planned   stop → stopped

5. 불규칙 동사 (*p.120 불규칙 동사 변화표 참조)

   eat → ate   have → had   go → went

LET'S CHECK

A ( ) 안에서 알맞은 말을 고르세요.

0 I (meet, (met)) Tom every day last week.

1 Cindy (buys, bought) a pair of jeans yesterday.

2 Bees (collect, collected) honey from flowers.

3 January (is, was) the first month of the year.

4 The *Titanic* (sinks, sank) in 1912.

5 Peter (writes, wrote) two books last year.

6 The postman (delivers, delivered) mail every day.

7 Ann's birthday (is, was) the day after her mom's.

8 My grandfather (pass, passed) away two years ago.

9 Nick (misses, missed) the school bus this morning.

B 주어진 문장을 ( ) 안의 지시대로 바꿔 쓰세요. (줄임말을 쓸 것)

0 The weather was good last weekend. (부정문)

→ _____ The weather wasn't good last weekend. _____

1 They were busy on Monday. (의문문)

→ _____

2 We went to the baseball game yesterday. (부정문)

→ _____

3 You enjoyed the movie. (의문문)

→ _____

4 He got a haircut yesterday. (의문문)

→ _____

WORDS A jeans 청바지 bee 벌 collect 모으다, 수집하다 sink 가라앉다 postman 우체부 deliver 배달하다 pass away 돌아가시다 miss 놓치다 B get a haircut 머리를 자르다

3 과거진행형

과거진행형은 '~하고 있었다, ~하는 중이었다'의 의미로 과거 특정 시점에 진행 중이었던 일을 나타낸다.

He **was driving** to work *at 8 o'clock this morning*.

I **was meeting** my friend *at that time*.

4 과거진행형의 형태

과거진행형은 주어의 인칭과 수에 따라 「be동사의 과거형 + 동사원형-ing」 형태로 쓴다.

긍정문	부정문	의문문
I **was reading**.	I **wasn't reading**.	**Was** I **reading**?
He **was working**.	He **wasn't working**.	**Was** he **working**?
They **were studying**.	They **weren't studying**.	**Were** they **studying**?

5 과거시제 vs. 과거진행형

과거시제는 과거에 이미 끝난 일을 나타낸다. 과거진행형은 과거 특정 시점에 동작이 진행 중이었음을 강조할 때 쓴다.

I **did** my homework *yesterday*.

A: What **were** you **doing** *at 9 o'clock*?

B: I **was doing** my homework.

6 현재진행형 vs. 과거진행형

현재진행형은 지금 진행 중인 동작을 나타낸다. 과거진행형은 과거 특정 시점에 진행 중이었던 동작을 나타낸다.

It **is raining** *right now*.

It **was raining** *an hour ago*.

LET'S CHECK

C   주어진 문장을 과거진행형으로 바꿔 쓰세요.

0   I wrote a letter.   →   I _____was writing_____ a letter.

1   Sam helped his mother.   →   Sam _____ his mother.

2   The doorbell rang.   →   The doorbell _____.

3   The kids jumped rope.   →   The kids _____ rope.

4   My friends ran.   →   My friends _____.

5   Bill played the guitar.   →   Bill _____ the guitar.

6   The cat drank milk.   →   The cat _____ milk.

7   They had breakfast.   →   They _____ breakfast.

8   We cleaned the house.   →   We _____ the house.

9   Mom made soup.   →   Mom _____ soup.

D   ( ) 안의 말을 이용하여 과거진행형 부정문과 의문문을 완성하세요. (줄임말을 쓸 것)

0   He _____wasn't sitting_____ on the bench. (not, sit)

1   I _____ for a bus. (not, wait)

2   We _____ the soccer game. (not, watch)

3   The boys _____. (not, fight)

4   Joe _____ socks. (not, wear)

5   _____ she _____ a walk? (take)

6   _____ the man _____ a newspaper? (buy)

7   _____ they _____ in the pool? (swim)

8   _____ you _____ ice cream? (eat)

9   _____ your sister _____ her bike? (ride)

WORDS   **C** doorbell 초인종   jump rope 줄넘기를 하다   **D** bench 벤치   fight 싸우다   take a walk 산책하다
pool 수영장 (= swimming pool)

LET'S PRACTICE

A   ( ) 안에서 알맞은 말을 고르세요.

0   I ((love), loved) tea. I drink it every day.

1   The bus (arrives, arrived) 10 minutes ago.

2   Bob (is, was) a taxi driver. Now he (sell, sells) cars.

3   Nick and Rosa (get, got) married last year.

4   Jane (travels, traveled) to Europe in 2018.

5   I (am, was) meeting my friends at noon yesterday.

6   Look! They (are, were) painting on the ground.

7   I saw Peter this morning. He (is, was) going to school.

8   A: What is Jack doing?   B: He (is, was) talking to the teacher.

9   A: Why were you laughing?   B: I (am, was) reading a funny book.

B   어제 Tom이 한 일을 보고 보기에서 알맞은 말을 골라 과거진행형 문장을 완성하세요.

| 보기 | eat lunch | ~~brush his teeth~~ | read a book | play soccer |

0   Tom _____was brushing his teeth_____ at 7 o'clock.

1   He _____ at noon.

2   He _____ at 4 o'clock.

3   He _____ at 9 o'clock.

WORDS   A arrive 도착하다   get married 결혼하다   travel to ~로 여행하다   at noon 정오에   ground 땅, 땅바닥   laugh 웃다   funny 웃기는,
재미있는

C 빈칸에 did/didn't, was/wasn't, were/weren't 중 알맞은 것을 넣어 대화를 완성하세요.

0 A: _____Did_____ you go to the concert last night?

B: Yes, I _____did_____. It _____was_____ very exciting.

1 A: _____ Lucy writing a letter?

B: No, she _____. She _____ drawing a picture.

2 A: _____ Jason and David studying?

B: Yes, they _____. They _____ studying math.

3 A: _____ you watch the soccer game last night?

B: No, I _____. I _____ sleeping at that time.

4 A: _____ you take a lot of photos in Greece?

B: No, I _____. I _____ have my camera.

D 밑줄 친 부분을 바르게 고치세요.

0 It <u>snows</u> a lot last winter. → *snowed*

1 The baby <u>sleeping</u> an hour ago. →

2 Sally <u>isn't</u> at home yesterday. →

3 Mr. Lee <u>wasn't</u> teach my class last year. →

4 Did you <u>met</u> your friends yesterday? →

5 We were <u>walk</u> to the subway station. →

6 Dave <u>didn't</u> sitting next to me then. →

7 They <u>move</u> to a new house last week. →

8 Did Mike <u>runs</u> to school this morning? →

9 <u>Were</u> they catch the bank robber? →

WORDS C concert 콘서트, 연주회 exciting 신나는, 흥미진진한 D subway station 지하철역 move 옮기다, 이사하다 catch 잡다
robber 강도

STEP 1

빈칸 완성 보기에서 알맞은 말을 골라 적절한 형태로 바꾸어 문장을 완성하세요.

| 보기 | be | know | invent | stand | wear |

1 나는 교복을 입는다.

→ I _____ a school uniform.

2 그는 1876년에 전화기를 발명했다.

→ He _____ the telephone in 1876.

3 그들은 버스 정류장에 서 있다.

→ They are _____ at the bus stop.

4 별들이 밝게 빛나고 있었다.

→ The stars _____ shining brightly.

5 그 여자는 나를 알고 있다.

→ The woman _____ me.

STEP 2

어구 배열 우리말과 일치하도록 ( ) 안의 말을 알맞게 배열하세요.

6 나의 조부모님은 시골에 사신다. (my, country, live, the, grandparents, in)

→ _____

7 나는 한 시간 전에 숙제를 끝냈다. (finished, ago, my, hour, an, I, homework)

→ _____

8 그는 인터넷 서핑을 하고 있었다. (was, the, surfing, Internet, he)

→ _____

9 Jessica는 꽃에 물을 주고 있다. (is, flowers, Jessica, watering, the)

→ _____

10 나는 영어를 잘 하지 못했다. (I, speak, didn't, well, English)

→ _____

영작하기 ( ) 안의 말을 이용하여 우리말을 영어로 옮기세요.

11 나의 할머니는 올해 70세이시다. (my grandmother, 70 years old, this year)

→ _____

12 그는 작년에 우리 체육 선생님이셨다. (my P.E. teacher, last year)

→ _____

13 그들은 금요일마다 외식을 한다. (eat out, on Fridays)

→ _____

14 우리 가족은 지난 주말에 소풍을 갔다. (my family, go on a picnic, last weekend)

→ _____

15 나는 귀신을 믿지 않는다. (believe in, ghosts)

→ _____

16 너는 어제 새 컴퓨터를 샀니? (buy, a new computer, yesterday)

→ _____

17 Tom은 그의 친구들을 기다리고 있다. (wait for, his friends)

→ _____

18 그 아이들은 보드게임을 하고 있었다. (the children, play, a board game)

→ _____

19 그녀는 피아노를 연습하고 있니? (practice, the piano)

→ _____

20 그들은 소파에 앉아있었니? (sit, on the sofa)

→ _____

REVIEW TEST
CHAPTER 01

[1-3] 빈칸에 들어갈 말로 알맞은 것을 고르시오.

1

Water _____ at 100°C.

① boil　　　　② boils
③ boiled　　　④ is boiling
⑤ was boiling

2

The train _____ 10 minutes ago.

① left　　　　② leave
③ leaves　　　④ leaving
⑤ is leaving

3

My father _____ TV at the moment.

① watch　　　② watches
③ watching　　④ is watching
⑤ was watching

서술형

[4-5] 다음 문장을 ( ) 안의 지시대로 바꿔 쓰시오.

4

The man has his I.D. card. (부정문)

→ The man _____ his I.D. card.

5

She was studying English last night. (의문문)

→ _____ English last night?

6 다음 문장을 현재진행형으로 바르게 바꾼 것은?

She cuts paper with scissors.

① She cutting paper with scissors.
② She is cutting paper with scissors.
③ She do cutting paper with scissors.
④ She was cutting paper with scissors.
⑤ She does cutting paper with scissors.

7 다음 우리말을 영어로 바르게 옮긴 것은?

그는 학교에 버스를 타고 갔니?

① Did he go to school by bus?
② Was he go to school by bus?
③ Did he going to school by bus?
④ Does he went to school by bus?
⑤ Was he going to school by bus?

8 빈칸에 들어갈 말이 나머지 넷과 <u>다른</u> 것은?

① I _____ very busy last weekend.
② Bill _____ late for school yesterday.
③ Jane _____ at home two hours ago.
④ He _____ taking a bowling class now.
⑤ She _____ going to school at 8 o'clock yesterday.

9 빈칸에 들어갈 말이 순서대로 바르게 짝지어진 것은?

> I _____ tall in elementary school. Now I _____ very tall.

① didn't – do ② didn't – am

③ wasn't – am ④ wasn't – was

⑤ am not – am

10 빈칸에 공통으로 들어갈 말은?

> A: Peter, _____ you find your key yesterday?
> B: Yes, I _____. It was in my bag.

① do ② are

③ did ④ were

⑤ does

[11-12] 밑줄 친 부분이 옳은 것을 고르시오.

11 ① Allen is having a dog.

② I'm wanting a cup of tea.

③ Are you knowing my name?

④ She is liking her new school.

⑤ They are having lunch together.

12 ① Chickens not fly high.

② The shop isn't sell shoes.

③ Does your brother run fast?

④ You didn't cleaned your room.

⑤ They don't eating popcorn now.

서술형

[13-14] 밑줄 친 부분을 바르게 고치시오.

13

> I visit my grandparents last weekend.

→ _____

14

> Do you make cupcakes now?

→ _____

서술형

[15-17] 우리말과 일치하도록 ( ) 안의 말을 이용하여 문장을 완성하시오.

15

> 그 엘리베이터는 2층에 서지 않는다. (stop)

→ The elevator _____ on the second floor.

16

> 그 소녀들은 기뻐서 뛰고 있었다. (jump)

→ The girls _____ for joy.

17

> 그는 어제 물고기를 많이 잡았니? (catch)

→ _____ a lot of fish yesterday?

CHAPTER
02

Present Perfect
현재완료

LET'S LOOK

I have washed the dishes.

The rain has stopped.

현재완료는 과거 한 시점에 일어난 일이 완료되었거나 현재까지 계속되는 상태임을 나타낸다. 현재완료는 「have/has + 과거분사」의 형태이며, 의미에 따라 **완료**, **경험**, **계속**, **결과** 용법으로 나뉜다.

UNIT 03

현재완료 1
Present Perfect 1

1 현재완료

현재완료는 과거 한 시점에 일어난 일이 완료되었거나 현재까지 계속되는 상태임을 나타낸다.

He **is going to wash**
his hands.

He **is washing**
his hands.

He **has washed**
his hands.

2 현재완료의 형태

❶ 긍정문은 「have/has + 과거분사」 형태로 쓴다. 부정문은 have/has 뒤에 not을 붙인다.

긍정문			부정문		
I/You/We/They	have (= 've)	과거분사	I/You/We/They	have not (= haven't)	과거분사
He/She/It	has (= 's)		He/She/It	has not (= hasn't)	

I **have finished** my homework.

My friend **has moved** to Vancouver.

I'm really hungry. I **haven't eaten** yet.

The banana **has not turned** yellow.

❷ 의문문은 「Have/Has + 주어 + 과거분사?」 형태로 쓴다.

의문문			긍정의 대답	부정의 대답
Have	I/you/we/they	과거분사?	Yes, 주어 + have.	No, 주어 + haven't.
Has	he/she/it		Yes, 주어 + has.	No, 주어 + hasn't.

A: **Have you packed** your bag?

B: **Yes, I have. / No, I haven't.**

A: **Has James scored** a goal?

B: **Yes, he has. / No, he hasn't.**

LET'S CHECK

A   주어진 문장이 과거시제인지 현재완료인지 고르세요.

		과거시제	현재완료
0	Tony has broken the window.	☐	☑
1	I had a bad cold last week.	☐	☐
2	We have visited the aquarium twice.	☐	☐
3	Have you eaten all the cookies?	☐	☐
4	Dad came home from work an hour ago.	☐	☐
5	Have you brushed your teeth?	☐	☐
6	Did it rain last night?	☐	☐
7	Joe bought a new computer yesterday.	☐	☐
8	The milk has gone bad.	☐	☐

B   주어진 문장을 (　) 안의 지시대로 바꿔 쓰세요.

0   Tom has locked the door. (부정문)

→   Tom hasn't locked the door.

1   Emma has found her book. (의문문)

→ _____

2   I have driven a car before. (부정문)

→ _____

3   You have seen my bag. (의문문)

→ _____

4   They have gone to Spain. (의문문)

→ _____

WORDS   A break 깨다   aquarium 수족관   go bad (음식이) 상하다   B lock 잠그다   find 찾다

3 과거분사의 형태

규칙 동사	과거형과 과거분사형이 같음	live – lived – **lived** study – studied – **studied**	work – worked – **worked** stop – stopped – **stopped**
불규칙 동사	A-B-C형	do – did – **done** go – went – **gone** sing – sang – **sung**	eat – ate – **eaten** see – saw – **seen** write – wrote – **written**
	A-B-B형	build – built – **built** leave – left – **left** sleep – slept – **slept**	have – had – **had** meet – met – **met** teach – taught – **taught**
	A-B-A형	come – came – **come**	run – ran – **run**
	A-A-A형	cut – cut – **cut** put – put – **put**	hit – hit – **hit** read – read – **read**

(*p.120 불규칙 동사 변화표 참조)

Peggy **has lived** in Seoul since 2018.

I **haven't seen** her for a month.

We**'ve** already **had** our breakfast.

Have you ever **run** in a marathon?

Daniel **has cut** his finger with a knife.

✔ NOTE   read의 과거형과 과거분사형은 [réd]로 읽는다.

I **read** books every day.
[riːd]

I have **read** the book twice.
[réd]

LET'S CHECK

C 주어진 동사의 과거형과 과거분사형을 쓰세요.

	현재	과거	과거분사		현재	과거	과거분사
0	see	saw	seen	20	build		
1	eat			21	send		
2	give			22	leave		
3	fall			23	lose		
4	take			24	sleep		
5	drive			25	feel		
6	ride			26	meet		
7	hide			27	sit		
8	break			28	win		
9	speak			29	sell		
10	get			30	hear		
11	wear			31	find		
12	grow			32	buy		
13	throw			33	catch		
14	drink			34	teach		
15	sing			35	come		
16	swim			36	run		
17	go			37	cut		
18	have			38	hit		
19	make			39	read		

WORDS C fall 떨어지다   ride 타다   hide 숨기다   grow 자라다; 재배하다   throw 던지다   build 짓다   leave 떠나다, 출발하다   lose 잃다; 지다
hear 듣다

LET'S PRACTICE

A ( ) 안에서 알맞은 말을 고르세요.

0   Judy hasn't (did, (done)) her homework yet.

1   The bus has already (come, came).

2   The mouse has (ran, run) away.

3   Brian hasn't (ate, eaten) his vegetables.

4   The monkey has (fallen, fell) from the tree.

5   She has (been, was) to New Zealand twice.

6   I have (knew, known) Mike for five years.

7   Everyone has (gave, given) Jane a present.

8   Larry has (saw, seen) the movie twice.

9   She has (written, wrote) many books for children.

B 그림을 보고 ( ) 안의 말을 이용하여 현재완료 문장을 완성하세요.

0  1  2  3

0   I _____haven't cleaned_____ my bedroom. (clean)

1   Sam _____ his arm. (break)

2   The train _____ the station. (leave)

3   The kids _____ their Christmas presents. (open)

WORDS   A run away 도망치다   present 선물   B arm 팔

C

( ) 안의 말을 이용하여 현재완료 의문문과 대답을 완성하세요.

0   A: _____Have_____ you ___finished___ your breakfast? (finish)

   B: Yes, I _____have_____ .

1   A: _____ Mr. Smith _____ his flight? (miss)

   B: No, he _____ .

2   A: _____ she _____ a lot of friends at her new school? (make)

   B: Yes, she _____ .

3   A: _____ your father _____ a new car? (buy)

   B: No, he _____ .

4   A: _____ they _____ the dishes? (wash)

   B: Yes, they _____ .

D

밑줄 친 부분을 바르게 고치세요.

0   Sara and John <u>has</u> passed the exam.   →   *have*

1   Have you <u>meet</u> the new teacher?   →

2   My best friend <u>was</u> gone to America.   →

3   Peter <u>haven't</u> found his bike.   →

4   The game <u>didn't</u> started for hours.   →

5   They <u>have watched not</u> the news.   →

6   <u>Did</u> you ever eaten lobster?   →

7   Have you <u>readed</u> *Treasure Island*?   →

8   Bill has <u>losed</u> a lot of weight.   →

WORDS   C flight 비행기, 항공편   D lobster 랍스터, 바닷가재   lose weight 살이 빠지다, 살을 빼다

UNIT 04

현재완료 2
Present Perfect 2

1 현재완료의 쓰임

❶ 완료 (~했다, ~한 상태이다)

어떤 일이 최근에 또는 막 완료된 상태임을 나타낸다. 주로 just(방금, 막), already(이미, 벌써), yet(아직) 등과 함께 쓰인다.

I **have** *just* **finished** my homework.

They **have** *already* **arrived**.

The movie **hasn't started** *yet*.

❷ 경험 (~해 본 적이 있다)

현재까지의 경험을 나타낸다. 주로 ever, never, before, once/twice/many times 등과 함께 쓰인다.

Have you *ever* **eaten** an insect?

My cousin lives in Thailand. He **has** *never* **seen** snow.

I **have heard** his name *before*.

Sally **has been** to Spain *twice*.

❸ 계속 (~해 왔다)

과거부터 현재까지 계속되는 일을 나타낸다. 주로 for, since, how long과 함께 쓰인다.

My parents **have lived** in Busan *for 10 years*. 〈for+기간: ~ 동안〉

Bob **has worked** at the bank *since 2017*. 〈since+과거 시점: ~부터〉

How long **has** she **played** the piano? 〈How long+현재완료?: ~한 지 얼마나 되었니?〉

❹ 결과 (~해 버렸다, 그래서 지금 ~하다)

과거에 일어난 일의 결과가 현재까지 영향을 미치는 상태를 나타낸다. 주로 go, lose, leave 등의 동사와 함께 쓰인다.

I **have lost** my notebook. (= I don't have it now.)

My sister **has gone** shopping. (= She isn't at home now.)

> **📝 NOTE** **been vs. gone**
> 1. have been (to): ~에 가 본 적이 있다 〈경험〉
>   She has been to Europe. 그녀는 유럽에 가 본 적이 있다.
> 2. have gone (to): ~에 가고 (지금 여기에) 없다. 〈결과〉
>   She has gone to Europe. 그녀는 지금 유럽에 가고 없다.

LET'S CHECK

A 주어진 현재완료 문장의 쓰임으로 알맞은 것을 고르세요

0	The package has just arrived.	☑ 완료	☐ 계속
1	Have you ever ridden a horse?	☐ 경험	☐ 결과
2	Chris has already left home.	☐ 완료	☐ 경험
3	He has worked here since last April.	☐ 완료	☐ 계속
4	I have been to Jejudo twice.	☐ 경험	☐ 결과
5	It hasn't rained for a month.	☐ 경험	☐ 계속
6	James has never had a pet.	☐ 경험	☐ 계속
7	Bill has lost his shoes.	☐ 경험	☐ 결과
8	How long have you learned English?	☐ 계속	☐ 결과
9	They have gone to school.	☐ 경험	☐ 결과

B 빈칸에 since 또는 for를 쓰세요.

0	_____since_____	1990
1	_____	three days
2	_____	yesterday
3	_____	two weeks
4	_____	a month
5	_____	last month
6	_____	3 o'clock
7	_____	an hour
8	_____	a long time
9	_____	two years ago

WORDS   A package 소포   pet 애완동물

2 현재완료 vs. 과거시제

❶ 현재완료는 사건이 발생한 시간이 중요하지 않다. 과거 특정 시점(yesterday, last week, two years ago, in 2017, when 등)이 올 경우에는 과거시제를 쓴다.

Dave **has finished** his homework. Dave는 그의 숙제를 끝낸 상태이다. (언제 끝났는지는 중요하지 않음)

Dave **finished** his homework *an hour ago*. Dave는 1시간 전에 그의 숙제를 끝냈다.

❷ 현재까지의 경험(~한 적이 있다)에 대해 말할 때는 현재완료를 쓴다. 과거 특정 시점에 있었던 일을 말할 때는 과거시제를 쓴다.

Have you *ever* **met** Cathy? 너는 Cathy를 만나 본 적이 있니?

Did you **meet** Cathy *yesterday*? 너는 어제 Cathy를 만났니?

I **have met** Cathy *once/twice/many times*. 나는 Cathy를 1번/2번/여러 번 만난 적이 있다.

I **met** Cathy *last year/two weeks ago/in 2015*. 나는 작년에/2주 전에/2015년에 Cathy를 만났다.

❸ 현재완료는 과거부터 현재까지 계속되는 일을 나타낼 수 있다. 과거시제는 과거에 이미 끝난 일을 나타내며, 현재까지 그 일이 계속되는지는 알 수가 없다.

Ann **has lived** here *for five years*. Ann은 여기서 5년째 살고 있다. (지금도 살고 있음)

Ann **lived** here *for five years*. Ann은 여기서 5년 동안 살았다. (지금은 어디에 사는지 모름)

LET'S CHECK

C ( ) 안에서 알맞은 말을 고르세요.

0   Mary ((made), has made) a cake yesterday.

1   My parents (lived, have lived) in this house since 2010.

2   This is a great book. I (read, have read) it many times.

3   (Did you watch, Have you watched) that TV show last night?

4   How long (did Mr. Smith teach, has Mr. Smith taught) English so far?

5   They (left, have left) school 30 minutes ago.

6   When (did you finish, have you finished) your homework?

7   My cousin lives in L.A. I (was, have been) there once.

8   The plane (landed, has landed) at the airport at 10:30.

D 주어진 동사의 과거형 또는 현재완료형을 써서 문장을 완성하세요.

0   go   (1) Emily _____has gone_____ to France.

            (2) Emily _____went_____ to France a week ago.

1   live   (1) We _____ here since 2015.

            (2) We _____ here in 2015.

2   be   (1) My dog _____ sick since last night.

            (2) My dog _____ sick last night.

3   eat   (1) I _____ Indian food twice.

            (2) I _____ Indian food last week.

4   not, read (1) He _____ my email yet.

            (2) He _____ my email yesterday.

LET'S PRACTICE

A 우리말과 일치하도록 빈칸에 알맞은 말을 넣어 문장을 완성하세요.

0 Jane은 방금 TV를 껐다.

→ Jane has _____just_____ turned off the TV.

1 우리는 이미 영화표를 샀다.

→ We have _____ bought the movie tickets.

2 그 페인트는 아직 마르지 않았다.

→ The paint hasn't dried _____.

3 나는 페루에 가 본 적이 한 번도 없다.

→ I have _____ been to Peru.

4 그녀는 10년째 영어를 가르치고 있다.

→ She has taught English _____ 10 years.

5 그는 중학교 때부터 안경을 써왔다.

→ He has worn glasses _____ middle school.

B 보기에서 알맞은 말을 골라 현재완료 의문문을 완성하세요. (단, 한 번씩만 쓸 것)

보기	~~be~~	eat	forget	meet	sleep	tell

0 Have you ever _____been_____ on TV?

1 Have you ever _____ in a tent?

2 Have you ever _____ a famous person?

3 Have you ever _____ strange food?

4 Have you ever _____ a lie to your parents?

5 Have you ever _____ something important?

WORDS A turn off 끄다 glasses 안경 B tent 텐트 famous 유명한 strange 이상한 lie 눕다; *거짓말 important 중요한

C 두 문장을 현재완료를 사용하여 한 문장으로 만드세요.

0 We became friends in kindergarten. We are still friends.

→ We ____*have*____ ____*been*____ friends since kindergarten.

1 Sally went to the library. She will be back in the evening.

→ Sally _____ _____ to the library.

2 Tim has a computer. He bought it five years ago.

→ Tim _____ _____ his computer for five years.

3 I watched the movie last weekend. I watched it today again.

→ I _____ _____ the movie twice.

4 David lost his student I.D. card. He can't find it anywhere.

→ David _____ _____ his student I.D. card.

D 밑줄 친 부분을 바르게 고치세요.

0 He has <u>gone</u> to London twice. → *been*

1 He <u>has lived</u> here from 2010 to 2014. →

2 I <u>have eaten never</u> this kind of pizza. →

3 Tim <u>had</u> a toothache since last week. →

4 Kelly has studied French <u>for</u> last year. →

5 <u>Did they have</u> done their work? →

6 <u>Did you</u> ever seen a panda? →

7 <u>I have met</u> Susan yesterday. →

8 She <u>hasn't sleep</u> well last night. →

WORDS   C kindergarten 유치원   student I.D. card 학생증   D toothache 치통

STEP 1

빈칸 완성 ( ) 안의 말을 이용하여 문장을 완성하세요.

1 Mike는 여기서 2015년부터 일해왔다. (work)

→ Mike _____ _____ here since 2015.

2 Kate는 벌써 그녀의 숙제를 끝냈다. (finish)

→ Kate _____ already _____ her homework.

3 너는 유럽에 가 본 적이 있니? (be)

→ _____ _____ ever _____ to Europe?

4 Susan은 지금 캐나다에 가고 없다. (go)

→ Susan _____ _____ to Canada.

5 나는 그 소설을 아직 읽지 않았다. (read)

→ I _____ _____ the novel yet.

STEP 2

어구 배열 우리말과 일치하도록 ( ) 안의 말을 알맞게 배열하세요.

6 우리는 5년째 서로 알고 지내고 있다. (for, known, five, have, each other, we, years)

→ _____

7 Steve는 방금 그 파일을 열어보았다. (just, has, Steve, opened, file, the)

→ _____

8 너는 태국 음식을 먹어 본 적이 있니? (ever, Thai food, eaten, you, have)

→ _____

9 나는 전에 그녀를 본 적이 한 번도 없다. (before, seen, I, never, have, her)

→ _____

10 누군가 내 가방을 가져갔다. (taken, somebody, my, has, bag)

→ _____

영작하기 ( ) 안의 말을 이용하여 우리말을 영어로 옮기세요. (현재완료를 사용할 것)

11 그들은 방금 역을 떠났다. (just, leave, the station)

→ _____

12 우리는 이미 그 소파를 팔았다. (already, sell, the sofa)

→ _____

13 Tim은 아직 그의 방을 청소하지 않았다. (clean, his room, yet)

→ _____

14 나는 전에 여기에 와 본 적이 있다. (be, here, before)

→ _____

15 그는 한 번도 해외여행을 해 본 적이 없다. (never, travel abroad)

→ _____

16 우리는 그 식당에서 여러 번 식사를 해봤다. (eat, at the restaurant, many times)

→ _____

17 Chris는 다리가 부러졌다. (break, his leg)

→ _____

18 우리 엄마는 운전면허 시험에 합격했다. (my mom, pass, her driving test)

→ _____

19 그는 2014년부터 차를 운전해왔다. (drive, a car, 2014)

→ _____

20 우리는 10년째 좋은 친구이다. (be, good friends, 10 years)

→ _____

REVIEW TEST
CHAPTER 02

1 동사의 과거형과 과거분사형이 잘못 연결된 것은?

① run – ran – run
② see – saw – seen
③ build – built – built
④ come – came – came
⑤ stop – stopped – stopped

[2-4] 빈칸에 들어갈 말로 알맞은 것을 고르시오.

2

My father has _____ a book before.

① write   ② writes   ③ wrote
④ writing   ⑤ written

3

_____ Tom missed the bus?

① Is   ② Did   ③ Has
④ Was   ⑤ Have

4

They have stayed in the pool _____ 9 o'clock.

① at   ② to   ③ for
④ from   ⑤ since

[5-6] 다음 두 문장을 한 문장으로 만들 때 빈칸에 알맞은 말을 쓰시오.

5

Eric lost his umbrella. He doesn't have it now.

→ Eric _____ _____ his umbrella.

6

I moved here five years ago. I still live here.

→ I _____ _____ here for five years.

7 다음 문장의 밑줄 친 부분과 쓰임이 같은 것은?

Have you ever eaten Mexican food?

① I haven't eaten lunch yet.
② The movie has just started.
③ The cat has broken my cup.
④ We have visited the zoo twice.
⑤ I have waited for him for an hour.

8 다음 우리말을 영어로 바르게 옮긴 것은?

나는 전에 뉴욕에 가 본 적이 있다.

① I went to New York before.
② I was been to New York before.
③ I was gone to New York before.
④ I have been to New York before.
⑤ I have gone to New York before.

9 빈칸에 들어갈 말이 순서대로 바르게 짝지어진 것은?

> · We _____ in class since this morning.
> · I _____ the book two days ago.

① are – read

② were – read

③ were – have read

④ have been – read

⑤ have been – have read

10 대화의 빈칸에 들어갈 말로 알맞은 것은?

> A: How long have you studied English?
> B: _____.

① Yes, I have.

② No, I am not.

③ For five years.

④ Three times a week.

⑤ I learned it at school.

[11-12] 다음 중 어법상 옳은 문장을 고르시오.

11 ① It have rained for a week.

② My father has wash his car.

③ I haven't never met her parents.

④ He has become a teacher in 2016.

⑤ She has played the piano for ten years.

12 ① When has the game started?

② I have seen the movie last week.

③ My friend has been sick yesterday.

④ The train has already left the station.

⑤ She has lived in Seoul five years ago.

서술형

[13-14] 어법상 틀린 부분을 찾아 바르게 고치시오.

13
> Mr. Kim has visited Korea in 2017.

_____ → _____

14
> They didn't done their homework yet.

_____ → _____

서술형

[15-17] 우리말과 일치하도록 ( ) 안의 말을 이용하여 문장을 완성하시오.

15
> 우리는 이미 그 소식을 들었다. (already, hear)

→ We _____ the news.

16
> 나는 오랫동안 그를 알고 지내고 있다. (know)

→ I _____ him for a long time.

17
> 지호는 학교에 늦은 적이 한 번도 없다. (never, be)

→ Jiho _____ late for school.

CHAPTER
03

To-Infinitives, Gerunds
To부정사, 동명사

LET'S LOOK

I want **to travel** around the world.

She enjoys **drawing**.

to부정사는 「to + 동사원형」 형태로 동사가 문장에서 **명사, 형용사, 부사**처럼 쓰이는 것이다. 품사가 정해지지 않았기 때문에 부정사(不定 부정 = 정해지지 않음)라고 부른다.

동명사는 「동사원형 + -ing」 형태로 동사가 문장에서 **명사**의 역할을 하는 것이다.

05 To부정사
To-Infinitives

1 to부정사

to부정사는 「to + 동사원형」의 형태이며, 동사가 문장에서 명사, 형용사, 부사처럼 쓰이는 것이다. to부정사는 쓰임에 따라 해석이 달라지므로 주의해야 한다.

I like **to sing**. 나는 <u>노래하는 것</u>을 좋아한다. 〈명사〉

We have many things **to do**. 우리는 <u>할</u> 일이 많다. 〈형용사〉

He came **to see** me yesterday. 그는 어제 나를 <u>보기 위해</u> 왔다. 〈부사〉

2 명사처럼 쓰이는 to부정사

'~하는 것'으로 해석되며 문장에서 주어, 목적어, 보어 역할을 한다.

❶ 주어 역할: ~하는 것은

to부정사(구)가 주어로 쓰일 경우 단수로 취급하여 단수동사를 쓴다.

To exercise every day *is* difficult.

To live in a big city *is* expensive.

> **⁄ NOTE** 주어로 쓰인 to부정사(구)는 주로 it으로 대신하고 문장 맨 뒤로 보낸다. 이때 it을 가주어, to부정사(구)를 진주어라고 한다. 가주어 it은 형식상의 주어이므로 '그것'이라고 해석하지 않는다.
>
> **To swim in the lake** is dangerous.
> = **It** is dangerous **to swim in the lake**.

❷ 목적어 역할: ~하는 것을, ~하기를

to부정사는 want, need, plan, decide, like, start 등의 동사 뒤에서 목적어로 쓰인다.

I *want* **to learn** a new language.

Mike *decided* **to buy** a used car.

We *hope* **to see** you soon.

❸ 보어 역할: ~하는 것(이다)

주로 be동사 뒤에 쓰여 주어를 보충 설명한다.

My dream *is* **to be** a cartoonist.

His goal *is* **to finish** school.

LET'S CHECK

A 밑줄 친 to부정사의 역할로 알맞은 것을 보기에서 고르세요.

| 보기 | ⓐ 주어 | ⓑ 목적어 | ⓒ 보어 |

0 <u>To get</u> up early is not easy for me. → ⓐ

1 I need <u>to buy</u> a new jacket. →

2 Amy decided <u>to change</u> schools. →

3 His job is <u>to deliver</u> pizza. →

4 Tony wants <u>to go</u> to bed now. →

5 His goal is <u>to open</u> a restaurant. →

6 It is hard <u>to solve</u> this puzzle. →

7 <u>To eat</u> healthy food is important. →

B ( ) 안에서 알맞은 말을 고르세요.

0 (Plant, (To plant)) trees is good for the environment.

1 We are planning to (go, going) to the zoo.

2 Her dream is to (is, be) a musical actress.

3 (To give, To giving) a speech is difficult.

4 Angela likes to (ate, eat) strawberry ice cream.

5 We decided to (join, joined) the club.

6 It is exciting (watch, to watch) a soccer game.

7 My goal is (speak, to speak) English well.

8 Andy wants to (stay, stayed) at home tonight.

9 Everyone needs to (wear, wears) a life jacket.

WORDS A change schools 전학하다 solve a puzzle 수수께끼를 풀다 healthy 건강한; *건강에 좋은 B plant 심다 environment 환경
actress 여배우 give a speech 연설하다 life jacket 구명조끼

3 형용사처럼 쓰이는 to부정사

'~할, ~하는'으로 해석되며 명사나 대명사를 뒤에서 꾸며준다.

Sumi has many *books* **to read**.

I have a lot of *homework* **to do**.

They need *something* **to drink**.

It is *time* **to go** to bed.

4 부사처럼 쓰이는 to부정사

주로 동사나 형용사를 꾸며주어 목적, 감정의 원인 등을 나타낸다.

❶ 목적: ~하기 위해

We *waited* in line **to get** on the bus.

He *went* to the teacher **to ask** a question.

To pass the exam, they *studied* hard.

❷ 감정의 원인: ~해서, ~하니

I'm *sorry* **to hear** the news.

She was *happy* **to find** her dog.

> **NOTE** 감정의 원인을 나타내는 to부정사 앞에 주로 쓰이는 형용사
>
> | happy 행복한 | glad 기쁜 | excited 신나는, 흥분된 |
> | --- | --- | --- |
> | sad 슬픈 | sorry 유감인, 안타까운 | surprised 놀란 |

C 밑줄 친 to부정사가 꾸며주는 말에 동그라미 하세요.

0 I have (a story) to tell you.

1 The dog is looking for something to eat.

2 He is not a man to tell a lie.

3 I want a book to read.

4 Do you have some money to buy snacks?

5 It's your turn to cook dinner.

6 I have a question to ask you.

7 It is time to say goodbye.

8 Susie has a lot of friends to help her.

9 We have some water to drink.

D 보기에서 알맞은 말을 골라 문장을 완성하세요. (단, 한 번씩만 쓸 것)

보기	to return the books	~~to get some rest~~	to write an email

0 I stayed at home ___to get some rest___.

1 He turned on the computer _____.

2 Larry went to the library _____.

보기	to hear the noise	to read my card	to win a gold medal

3 My mother was happy _____.

4 The baby was surprised _____.

5 The swimmer was excited _____.

LET'S PRACTICE

A 밑줄 친 to부정사의 쓰임으로 알맞은 것을 고르세요.

0	He decided <u>to lose</u> weight.	☑ 명사	☐ 형용사	☐ 부사
1	My dream is <u>to be</u> an astronaut.	☐ 명사	☐ 형용사	☐ 부사
2	They need money <u>to buy</u> food.	☐ 명사	☐ 형용사	☐ 부사
3	I have some jeans <u>to wash</u>.	☐ 명사	☐ 형용사	☐ 부사
4	We went to sea <u>to see</u> the whales.	☐ 명사	☐ 형용사	☐ 부사
5	Ann was the first guest <u>to arrive</u>.	☐ 명사	☐ 형용사	☐ 부사
6	It is difficult <u>to understand</u> him.	☐ 명사	☐ 형용사	☐ 부사
7	I go to the park <u>to jog</u> every day.	☐ 명사	☐ 형용사	☐ 부사
8	John was happy <u>to find</u> a new job.	☐ 명사	☐ 형용사	☐ 부사

B 주어진 문장에서 to가 들어갈 곳에 모두 ✓로 표시하세요.

0   You need ✓take off your shoes.

1   I'm busy. I have a lot of work do.

2   I am glad see you again.

3   Do you want go to the beach?

4   Be a parent is not easy.

5   See is believe.

6   She hopes be a teacher.

7   We are going out eat dinner.

8   It is dangerous play with fire.

9   I'm so tired. I don't have enough time sleep.

WORDS   A astronaut 우주 비행사   whale 고래   guest 손님   understand 이해하다   jog 조깅하다   B take off 벗다   glad 기쁜, 반가운
play with fire 불장난을 하다   enough 충분한

C

그림을 보고 보기에서 알맞은 말을 골라 적절한 형태로 바꾸어 문장을 완성하세요.

0    1    2   3

| 보기 | catch | ~~play~~ | read | see |

0   It is fun _____to play_____ in the water.

1   She bought a magazine _____ on the plane.

2   They are running _____ the bus.

3   We were surprised _____ the building.

D

( ) 안의 말을 알맞게 배열하여 문장을 완성하세요.

0   (ride, roller coaster, to, a)

→ ___To ride a roller coaster___ is exciting.

1   (to, wanted, eat)

→ The child _____ the cake.

2   (to, is, have)

→ My wish _____ my own room.

3   (things, to, many, do)

→ Farmers have _____ in spring.

4   (a, buy, to, present)

→ He went to the shop _____ for his mother.

5   (help, happy, to)

→ I'm very _____ you.

WORDS   C catch 잡다; *(시간에 맞춰) 타다   D roller coaster 롤러코스터   wish 소원, 바람   own 자기 자신의   spring 봄

06 동명사
Gerunds

1 동명사

동명사는 「동사원형 + -ing」의 형태이며, 동사가 문장에서 명사처럼 쓰이는 것이다.

- be late 늦다   →   **being** late 늦는 것
- go home 집에 가다   →   **going** home 집에 가는 것
- make a decision 결정하다 →   **making** a decision 결정하는 것

2 동명사의 쓰임

'~하는 것'으로 해석되며 문장에서 주어, 목적어, 보어 역할을 한다.

❶ 주어 역할: ~하는 것은

동명사(구)가 주어로 쓰일 경우 단수로 취급하여 단수동사를 쓴다.

Learning *is* important.

Eating vegetables *is* good for your health.

> ✎NOTE   주어로 쓰이는 동명사는 to부정사로 바꿔 쓸 수 있다.
>
> **Riding** a bicycle is fun.
>
> = **To ride** a bicycle is fun. / **It** is fun **to ride** a bicycle.

❷ 목적어 역할: ~하는 것을, ~하기를

동명사는 enjoy, finish, keep, mind, start, like 등의 동사나 전치사 뒤에서 목적어로 쓰인다.

He *enjoys* **surfing** in the sea.

I *started* **learning** Chinese.

Judy is good *at* **drawing** animals.

Thank you *for* **helping** us.

❸ 보어 역할: ~하는 것(이다)

주로 be동사 뒤에 쓰여 주어를 보충 설명한다.

My favorite sport *is* **swimming**.

His job *is* **selling** clothes.

> ✎NOTE   보어로 쓰이는 동명사는 to부정사로 바꿔 쓸 수 있다.
>
> Love is **giving**. = Love is **to give**.

LET'S CHECK

A 보기에서 알맞은 말을 골라 동명사로 바꾸어 문장을 완성하세요. (단, 한 번씩만 쓸 것)

보기	buy	eat	~~ski~~	watch

0 _____Skiing_____ is a popular winter sport.

1 _____ TV is bad for your eyes.

2 _____ things on the Internet is convenient.

3 _____ fast food is not healthy.

보기	come	cook	play	read

4 Mary doesn't enjoy _____ . She usually eats out.

5 My dog likes _____ with a ball.

6 I finished _____ the book last night.

7 John keeps _____ to work late.

보기	be	drive	fix	learn

8 I'm sorry for _____ late.

9 Kevin is interested in _____ Korean.

10 My brother is good at _____ things.

11 She is afraid of _____ . She takes the subway to work.

보기	listen	make	teach

12 Her favorite activity is _____ to music.

13 My hobby is _____ model airplanes.

14 His job is _____ science at high school.

WORDS **A** popular 인기 있는, 대중적인 convenient 편리한 eat out 외식하다 keep -ing 계속 ~하다 fix 고치다, 수리하다 be interested in ~에 관심[흥미]이 있다 be good at ~을 잘하다 be afraid of ~을 두려워하다 model airplane 모형 비행기

3 동명사와 to부정사

동명사와 to부정사는 둘 다 동사의 목적어로 쓰일 수 있지만, 동사에 따라 목적어로 취하는 형태가 달라지므로 주의한다.

❶ 동명사를 목적어로 취하는 동사

enjoy 즐기다	finish 끝내다	practice 연습하다	동사원형 + -ing
mind 꺼리다	give up 그만두다	keep 계속하다	

He *enjoys* **helping** others.
Do you *mind* **opening** the window?
I *finished* **writing** the letter.

❷ to부정사를 목적어로 취하는 동사

want 원하다	need 필요하다	decide 결정하다	to + 동사원형
hope 희망하다	plan 계획하다	promise 약속하다	

I *want* **to be** a pilot.
Judy *hopes* **to go** to university.

❸ 동명사와 부정사 둘 다 목적어로 취하는 동사

like 좋아하다	begin 시작하다	hate 싫어하다	동사원형 + -ing / to + 동사원형
love 매우 좋아하다	start 시작하다	continue 계속하다	

I love **dancing.**
= I love **to dance.**

She hates **cleaning** the bathroom.
= She hates **to clean** the bathroom.

The baby started **crying.**
= The baby started **to cry.**

LET'S CHECK

B ( ) 안에서 알맞은 말을 <u>모두</u> 고르세요.

0 I need (getting, (to get)) a haircut.

1 Bob decided (quitting, to quit) his job.

2 Do you like (eating, to eat) Italian food?

3 The train started (moving, to move) again.

4 Joan finished (cooking, to cook) dinner.

5 Do you mind (waiting, to wait) for a minute?

6 He gave up (smoking, to smoke) a year ago.

7 The two girls kept (talking, to talk) in class.

8 Sally hopes (passing, to pass) the exam.

9 Andy hates (eating, to eat) broccoli.

10 It began (snowing, to snow) last night.

11 My mom loves (watching, to watch) old movies.

12 Do you want (leaving, to leave) now?

13 Joe promised (helping, to help) his mother.

14 I enjoy (reading, to read) in my free time.

15 We are planning (going, to go) hiking this weekend.

16 Paul is good at (memorizing, to memorize) names.

17 He will continue (studying, to study) after graduation.

18 We practice (playing, to play) soccer on Fridays.

19 I am thinking about (going, to go) to Europe next summer.

20 Thank you for (answering, to answering) my questions.

21 Debbie doesn't enjoy (going, to go) shopping.

22 My parents hope (living, to live) in the country someday.

WORDS   B quit 그만두다 for a minute 잠시 동안 memorize 암기하다 graduation 졸업 country 국가, 나라; *시골 someday 언젠가

LET'S PRACTICE

A 밑줄 친 동명사가 문장에서 하는 역할을 보기에서 고르세요.

보기	ⓐ 주어	ⓑ 목적어	ⓒ 보어

0 I don't enjoy <u>playing</u> computer games. → ⓑ

1 Have you finished <u>using</u> the printer? →

2 His bad habit is <u>shaking</u> his legs. →

3 <u>Talking</u> loudly in the library is rude. →

4 He doesn't mind <u>working</u> on the weekend. →

5 Her favorite hobby is <u>growing</u> plants. →

6 <u>Doing</u> the same thing every day is boring. →

7 My sister is thinking about <u>studying</u> abroad. →

B 두 문장의 뜻이 같도록 빈칸에 알맞은 말을 쓰세요.

0 To watch a baseball game is exciting.

= _____Watching_____ a baseball game is exciting.

1 His job is to design buildings.

= His job is _____ buildings.

2 She likes to listen to classical music.

= She likes _____ to classical music.

3 The workers started to move the boxes.

= The workers started _____ the boxes.

4 My friend speaks Chinese well.

= My friend is good at _____ Chinese.

WORDS A habit 습관 shake one's leg(s) 다리를 떨다 rude 무례한 boring 지루한 study abroad 외국에서 공부하다 B design 설계하다

C 그림을 보고 보기에서 알맞은 말을 골라 적절한 형태로 바꾸어 문장을 완성하세요.

0    1    2    3

| 보기 | open the door | buy a new car | go to the dentist | do her homework |

0 Steve wants ___to buy a new car___.

1 Julie finished _____ at midnight.

2 Do you mind _____ for me?

3 Mike needs _____.

D 밑줄 친 부분을 바르게 고치세요.

0 They want <u>play</u> basketball.   →   to play

1 My dad enjoys <u>to fish</u> in the lake.   →

2 I plan <u>taking</u> a computer course.   →

3 Jack promised <u>be</u> quiet in class.   →

4 Don't give up. Keep <u>tries</u>.   →

5 We are thinking about <u>to go</u> to Hawaii.   →

6 I don't mind <u>watch</u> the movie again.   →

7 Daniel is funny. He is good at <u>tells</u> jokes.   →

8 Thank you for <u>drive</u> me to school.   →

9 The school decided <u>building</u> a new pool.   →

WORDS   C go to the dentist 치과에 가다   midnight 자정   D course 수업   try 노력하다   joke 농담

STEP 1

빈칸 완성 보기에서 알맞은 말을 골라 적절한 형태로 바꾸어 문장을 완성하세요.

보기	be	go	show	watch	write

1 하루 종일 TV 보는 것은 지루하다.

→ It is boring _____ _____ TV all day.

2 그는 의사가 되기 위해 열심히 공부했다.

→ He studied hard _____ _____ a doctor.

3 너에게 보여줄 사진이 몇 장 있어.

→ I have some pictures _____ _____ you.

4 우리는 이번 주말에 캠핑을 가려고 계획 중이다.

→ We are planning _____ _____ camping this weekend.

5 나는 어젯밤에 그 보고서 쓰는 것을 끝냈다.

→ I finished _____ the report last night.

STEP 2

어구 배열 우리말과 일치하도록 ( ) 안의 말을 알맞게 배열하세요.

6 밤에 운전하는 것은 위험하다. (dangerous, is, night, driving, at)

→ _____

7 그의 직업은 새들을 연구하는 것이다. (study, job, his, to, birds, is)

→ _____

8 나뭇잎들이 떨어지기 시작했다. (began, fall, leaves, to)

→ _____

9 나는 오늘 밤에 해야 할 숙제가 있다. (homework, to, have, do, I)

→ _____ tonight.

10 사람들은 인사하기 위해 악수를 한다. (hello, people, shake, to, hands, say)

→ _____

STEP 3

영작하기 ( ) 안의 말을 이용하여 우리말을 영어로 옮기세요.

11 나는 좋은 성적을 받고 싶다. (want, get, good grades)

→ _____

12 그는 비밀을 지키겠다고 약속했다. (promise, keep, the secret)

→ _____

13 John은 그녀와 결혼하기로 결심했다. (decide, marry)

→ _____

14 나는 숲 속을 걷는 것을 매우 좋아한다. (love, walk, in the forest)

→ _____

15 나는 여가 시간에 영화 보는 것을 즐긴다. (enjoy, watch, movies, in my free time)

→ _____

16 그녀는 매일 영어로 말하는 것을 연습한다. (practice, speak, English, every day)

→ _____

17 그들은 계속 걸었다. (keep, walk)

→ _____

18 그는 읽을 책을 좀 샀다. (buy, some books, read)

→ _____

19 우리는 해돋이를 보기 위해 일찍 일어났다. (get up, early, see, the sunrise)

→ _____

20 Tom은 골을 넣어서 기뻤다. (happy, score, a goal)

→ _____

REVIEW TEST
CHAPTER 03

[1-3] 빈칸에 들어갈 말로 알맞은 것을 고르시오.

1

_____ is good exercise.

① Walk ② Walks ③ Walking
④ Walked ⑤ To walking

2

They were excited _____ the news.

① hear ② hears ③ hearing
④ to hear ⑤ to heard

3

Jake is good at _____ math problems.

① solve ② solves ③ solving
④ to solve ⑤ to solving

[4-5] 빈칸에 들어갈 말로 알맞지 않은 것을 고르시오.

4

We _____ to go on a picnic.

① hoped ② wanted ③ planned
④ enjoyed ⑤ decided

5

His job is _____.

① selling cars
② teach English
③ to deliver mail
④ fixing computers
⑤ to help sick people

6 두 문장의 뜻이 같도록 할 때 빈칸에 알맞은 것은?

To learn a new language is helpful.
→ _____ is helpful to learn a new language.

① It ② He ③ This
④ That ⑤ What

[7-8] 밑줄 친 부분의 쓰임이 나머지 넷과 다른 것을 고르시오.

7
① I have some letters to write.
② He has some clothes to wash.
③ It is your turn to clean the house.
④ We went to the park to play soccer.
⑤ Summer is the best season to swim.

8
① Telling lies is wrong.
② Thank you for inviting us.
③ He loves eating Korean food.
④ My sister is studying in her room.
⑤ My cat's favorite activity is sleeping.

9 빈칸에 들어갈 말이 순서대로 바르게 짝지어진 것은?

· He promised _____ us next month.

· Do you mind _____ the window?

① visit – open

② visiting – to open

③ visiting – opening

④ to visit – to open

⑤ to visit – opening

10 빈칸에 공통으로 들어갈 수 없는 것은?

· Susan _____ to learn Spanish.

· My brother _____ exercising.

① liked   ② hated   ③ began

④ started   ⑤ needed

11 밑줄 친 부분이 잘못된 것은?

① The baby kept crying all night.

② Paul decided buying a new car.

③ They practiced singing the song.

④ My brother enjoys playing sports.

⑤ I gave up eating sweets after meals.

12 밑줄 친 It의 쓰임이 나머지 넷과 다른 하나는?

① It is fun to ride a bicycle.

② It is easy to make spaghetti.

③ It is a difficult question to solve.

④ It takes time to download the file.

⑤ It is wonderful to have good friends.

서술형

[13-14] 어법상 틀린 부분을 찾아 바르게 고치시오.

13

We need to going home right now.

_____ → _____

14

Did you finish read the book?

_____ → _____

서술형

[15-16] 우리말과 일치하도록 ( ) 안의 말을 알맞게 배열하시오.

15

그 산을 등반하는 것은 어렵다.

(climbing, is, the, difficult, mountain)

→ _____

16

그는 음식을 살 돈이 없었다.

(have, he, money, didn't, buy, to, food)

→ _____

서술형

17 우리말과 일치하도록 ( ) 안의 말을 이용하여 문장을 완성하시오.

Nick은 새 자전거를 사기 위해 돈을 저축하고 있다.

(buy, a new bike)

→ Nick is saving money

_____ .

CHAPTER
04

Various Verbs
여러 가지 동사

LET'S LOOK

I **feel** sick.

Music **makes** her happy.

Mom **gave** me a present.

영어에는 다양한 동사들이 있다. 동사만으로는 의미가 불완전한 경우 주어나
목적어를 보충 설명해주는 **보어**를 필요로 하기도 하고, '～에게 …해주다'의 의미를 갖는
수여동사는 두 개의 목적어를 취하기도 한다. 동사의 종류에 따라 문장의 구조가
달라지므로 각 동사의 성격을 잘 파악해두도록 하자.

07 여러 가지 동사 1
Various Verbs 1

1 감각동사

다섯 가지 감각을 나타내는 동사로 look(~하게 보이다), feel(~하게 느껴지다), smell(~한 냄새가 나다), sound(~하게 들리다), taste(~한 맛이 나다)가 있다. 감각동사 뒤에는 주어의 성질, 상태를 설명해주는 형용사가 주격 보어로 쓰인다.

주어	감각동사	형용사
The girl	looks	happy.
The silk scarf	feels	soft.
The soup	smells	good.
Her voice	sounds	beautiful.
The watermelon	tastes	sweet.

NOTE 1. 감각동사 뒤에 부사를 쓰지 않도록 주의한다.

The girl **looks** *happily*. [×]   The soup **smells** *well*. [×]

2. 감각동사 뒤에 명사가 올 경우에는 동사 뒤에 전치사 like(~처럼)를 쓴다.

She **looks like** *a model*. 그녀는 모델처럼 보인다.
The ice cream **tastes like** *a melon*. 그 아이스크림은 멜론 맛이 난다.

2 목적격 보어가 필요한 동사

목적어의 성질, 상태를 설명해주는 목적격 보어가 필요한 동사로 make(~을 …하게 만들다), keep(~을 …하게 유지하다), find(~가 …라는 것을 알게 되다), elect(~을 …로 선출하다), call/name(~을 …라고 부르다/이름 짓다) 등이 있다. 이 동사들은 목적어 뒤에 형용사, 명사 등이 목적격 보어로 쓰인다.

주어	동사	목적어	목적격 보어
He	makes	me	happy.
She	keeps	her room	clean.
I	found	the book	interesting.
They	elected	her	president.
We	called/named	our dog	Leo.

+PLUS 목적격 보어는 형용사, 명사 외에도 동사에 따라 다양한 형태가 올 수 있다.

Tom **wanted** me *to go* with him. Tom은 내가 그와 함께 가기를 원했다. 〈to부정사〉
I **saw** her *playing* the piano. 나는 그녀가 피아노 치는 것을 보았다. 〈동명사〉
My brother **helps** me *do* my homework. 우리 형은 내가 숙제 하는 것을 도와준다. 〈동사원형〉

LET'S CHECK

A ( ) 안에서 알맞은 말을 고르세요.

0 Your sister looks ((smart), smartly).

1 The pizza tastes too (salt, salty).

2 The chicken curry smells (good, well).

3 My pillow feels (soft, softly).

4 The workers look very (busy, busily).

5 His voice (looks, sounds) angry.

6 Black coffee (feels, tastes) bitter.

7 The cheese (smells, sounds) very strong.

8 This muffin (smells, smells like) a banana.

9 The man next door (look, looks like) a nice person.

B 주어진 문장에서 목적어에는 동그라미 하고, 목적격 보어에는 밑줄을 치세요.

0 The invention made (him) rich.

1 Regular exercise keeps you healthy.

2 Linda found the math test difficult.

3 The bad food made the boy sick.

4 My grandma calls me Sweetie.

5 They named their daughter Julie.

6 We elected Dave the captain of our team.

7 Jennifer found the movie boring.

8 The cook made the soup spicy.

9 He made his youngest son the king.

WORDS   A bitter (맛이) 쓴   B invention 발명품   regular 규칙적인   captain 주장   cook 요리하다; *요리사   spicy (맛이) 매운

LET'S PRACTICE

A ( ) 안에서 알맞은 말을 골라 문장을 완성하세요. (필요하면 형태를 바꿀 것)

0 (look, feel)

(1) The princess _____looks_____ beautiful.

(2) Mike ate too much. Now he _____feels_____ sick.

1 (look, sound)

(1) Her new hairstyle _____ nice.

(2) Your idea _____ great.

2 (smell, taste)

(1) The pie in the oven _____ good.

(2) Yum! These cookies _____ delicious.

3 (feel, smell)

(1) This perfume _____ wonderful. I'll buy it.

(2) This wool blanket _____ warm. I can sleep well with it.

B 그림을 보고 보기에서 알맞은 말을 골라 ( ) 안의 말과 함께 써서 문장을 완성하세요. (단, 한 번씩만 쓸 것)

보기	look	~~smell~~	sound	taste

0 This rose _____smells sweet_____. (sweet)

1 His new car _____. (expensive)

2 These chicken legs _____. (fantastic)

3 Their music _____. (beautiful)

WORDS A oven 오븐 delicious 맛있는 perfume 향수 B sweet 달콤한; *향긋한, 향기로운

C   ( ) 안에서 알맞은 말을 고르세요.

0   My mistake (called, (made)) him angry.

1   We (found, elected) the class fun.

2   She (made, named) her brown puppy Coco.

3   The ice will (call, keep) the water cool.

4   They (called, kept) the firemen heroes.

5   This will make your job (easy, easily).

6   The teacher found the boy (bright, brightly).

7   Call me (your best friend, as your best friend).

8   They elected (him their leader, their leader him).

9   I found (useful the TV program, the TV program useful).

D   ( ) 안의 말을 알맞게 배열하여 문장을 완성하세요.

0   (I, the box, empty, found)

→ _____ I found the box empty. _____

1   (made, the song, her, famous)

→ _____

2   (keeps, Natasha, her kitchen, clean)

→ _____

3   (him, his friends, a genius, call)

→ _____

4   (the town, Mr. Brown, mayor, elected)

→ _____

WORDS   C mistake 실수   hero 영웅   bright 밝은; *영리한, 총명한   leader 지도자, 대표   useful 유용한   D empty 빈   genius 천재   mayor 시장

08 여러 가지 동사 2
Various Verbs 2

1 수여동사

수여동사는 '~에게 …해주다'의 의미를 가진 동사이다. 수여동사는 '~에게(간접목적어)'와
'…을(직접목적어)'에 해당하는 두 개의 목적어를 갖는다.

주어	동사	간접목적어(~에게)	직접목적어(…을)
Ann	gave	Tom	candy.
Mom	made	me	a cake.
Mr. Kim	asked	his students	a question.

2 수여동사의 문장 전환

수여동사가 쓰인 문장은 간접목적어와 직접목적어의 위치를 바꾸어 쓸 수 있다. 이 경우 간접목적어 앞에
전치사 to, for, of를 쓴다.

주어	동사	직접목적어	전치사	간접목적어
Ann	gave	candy	to	Tom.
Mom	made	a cake	for	me.
Mr. Kim	asked	a question	of	his students.

❶ 간접목적어 앞에 to를 쓰는 동사: give(주다), send(보내다), pass(건네주다), lend(빌려주다), show(보여주다),
bring(가져다 주다), tell(말하다), write(쓰다), teach(가르치다)

Judy **wrote** *her friend* a card.

→ Judy **wrote** a card **to** *her friend*.

❷ 간접목적어 앞에 for를 쓰는 동사: buy(사주다), get(가져다 주다), make(만들어주다)

My father **bought** *me* a new computer.

→ My father **bought** a new computer **for** *me*.

❸ 간접목적어 앞에 of를 쓰는 동사: ask(묻다)

He always **asks** *me* difficult questions.

→ He always **asks** difficult questions **of** *me*.

LET'S CHECK

A 주어진 문장에서 간접목적어에는 동그라미 하고, 직접목적어에는 밑줄을 치세요.

0   Bill showed (us) his toys.

1   My grandmother gave me some money.

2   Amy will buy her mom a present.

3   Tony made his parents breakfast.

4   Elli sent her friends Christmas cards.

5   I lent George my baseball glove.

6   Can you bring me some water?

7   Jake told us a funny story.

8   The man asked me my name.

9   Janet taught the children a song.

B 빈칸에 to, for, of 중 알맞은 전치사를 넣어 문장을 완성하세요.

0   He gave ten roses ____to____ her.

1   She showed the map _____ us.

2   I sent a text message _____ my friend.

3   Mr. Roger teaches math _____ students.

4   John brought some food _____ us.

5   Tom lent his bike _____ his friend.

6   She passed the sugar _____ me.

7   Robin made a house _____ his dog.

8   I bought a teddy bear _____ my sister.

9   The reporter asked some questions _____ him.

WORDS   A baseball glove 야구 글러브   B map 지도 reporter 기자

LET'S PRACTICE

A

밑줄 친 동사가 수여동사이면 O, 아니면 X를 쓰세요.

0   I gave Paul a birthday card.   O

1   He showed us his album.

2   She can read a book in English.

3   Sharks have sharp teeth.

4   My friends call me Cindy.

5   You can ask me any questions.

6   Jenny made Dad a cake.

7   The present made me happy.

8   We bought two tickets for the show.

9   My grandparents bought me nice shoes.

B

그림을 보고 보기에서 알맞은 말을 골라 (   ) 안의 말과 함께 써서 문장을 완성하세요. (단, 한 번씩만 쓸 것)

0	1	2	3

보기	asked	~~gave~~	made	showed

0   John _____gave his wife a ring_____. (his wife, a ring)

1   Mom _____. (me, pizza)

2   Brian _____. (Jane, his room)

3   She _____. (me, the way to the station)

WORDS   A album 앨범   shark 상어   sharp 날카로운   B the way to ~로 가는 길

C ( ) 안에서 알맞은 말을 고르세요.

0   Kelly gave an interesting book ((to), for) me.

1   Mr. Evans teaches English (of, to) us.

2   My mom won't buy a short skirt (to, for) me.

3   Mark asked a strange question (of, to) me.

4   I'll make a cup of tea (to, for) you.

5   Can you lend (me your pen, your pen me)?

6   I wrote (my cousin a postcard, a postcard my cousin).

7   Please pass (to me the ball, the ball to me).

8   He told (to everyone the news, the news to everyone).

9   The waiter brought (the menu me, the menu to me).

D 두 문장의 뜻이 같도록 빈칸에 알맞은 말을 써서 문장을 완성하세요.

0   He gave me some advice.

= He gave _____ some advice to me _____.

1   Kevin showed me his new camera.

= Kevin showed _____.

2   Tom bought us dinner.

= Tom bought _____.

3   Linda teaches her students yoga.

= Linda teaches _____.

4   Sally sent her friends invitations.

= Sally sent _____.

WORDS   C postcard 엽서   D advice 조언, 충고   invitation 초대장

STEP 1 〔빈칸 완성〕 보기에서 알맞은 말을 골라 적절한 형태로 바꾸어 문장을 완성하세요.

보기	call	feel	make	show	taste

1 그의 발은 차가웠다.

→ His feet _____ cold.

2 그 레모네이드는 맛이 달다.

→ The lemonade _____ sweet.

3 그 소식은 나를 슬프게 만들었다.

→ The news _____ me sad.

4 너는 나를 Eddie라고 불러도 돼.

→ You can _____ me Eddie.

5 Henry는 나에게 그의 가족 사진을 보여주었다.

→ Henry _____ me a photo of his family.

STEP 2 〔어구 배열〕 우리말과 일치하도록 ( ) 안의 말을 알맞게 배열하세요.

6 그 이야기는 이상하게 들린다. (the, strange, story, sounds)

→ _____

7 이 안전벨트는 당신을 안전하게 지켜줄 것이다. (this, keep, will, you, safe, seatbelt)

→ _____

8 우리는 Jack을 반장으로 선출했다. (we, class president, Jack, elected)

→ _____

9 그녀는 나에게 아무 것도 말하지 않았다. (didn't, tell, she, me, anything)

→ _____

10 엄마는 내 친구들에게 쿠키를 만들어주셨다. (made, Mom, friends, cookies, my, for)

→ _____

STEP 3

영작하기 ( ) 안의 말을 이용하여 우리말을 영어로 옮기세요.

11 그 남자는 완벽해 보인다. (the man, look, perfect)

→ _____

12 이 샴푸는 향기로운 냄새가 난다. (this shampoo, smell, sweet)

→ _____

13 그것은 흥미로운 생각처럼 들린다. (that, sound, an interesting idea)

→ _____

14 그 모닥불은 우리를 따뜻하게 해주었다. (the campfire, keep, warm)

→ _____

15 그녀는 기말고사가 어렵다는 것을 알게 되었다. (find, the final exam, difficult)

→ _____

16 나는 내 자전거를 Fred라고 이름 지었다. (name, my bike, Fred)

→ _____

17 책은 우리에게 많은 정보를 준다. (books, give, a lot of information)

→ _____

18 그 웨이터는 나에게 물 한잔을 가져다주었다. (the waiter, bring, a glass of water)

→ _____

19 Jackie는 학생들에게 음악을 가르친다. (teach, music, students, to)

→ _____

20 그는 나에게 몇 가지 질문을 했다. (ask, some question, me, of)

→ _____

[1-3] 빈칸에 들어갈 말로 알맞지 <u>않은</u> 것을 고르시오.

1

This song sounds _____.

① nice   ② well   ③ great
④ strange   ⑤ beautiful

2

Andy _____ the soccer ball to me.

① gave   ② sent   ③ showed
④ passed   ⑤ bought

3

The movie made her _____.

① rich   ② sadly   ③ happy
④ sleepy   ⑤ famous

4 밑줄 친 부분이 <u>잘못된</u> 것은?

① The milk <u>tastes bad</u>.
② Your idea <u>sounds good</u>.
③ The soup <u>smells chicken</u>.
④ The picture <u>looks wonderful</u>.
⑤ This armchair <u>feels comfortable</u>.

5 다음 우리말을 영어로 바르게 옮긴 것은?

Susan은 나에게 샌드위치를 만들어주었다.

① Susan made a sandwich me.
② Susan made to me a sandwich.
③ Susan made a sandwich to me.
④ Susan made for me a sandwich.
⑤ Susan made a sandwich for me.

서술형

[6-8] ( ) 안의 말을 넣어 문장을 다시 쓰시오.

6

Mr. Lee teaches science. (us)

→ _____

7

She found the boy. (honest)

→ _____

8

The school elected student of the year. (him)

→ _____

9 빈칸에 들어갈 말이 순서대로 바르게 짝지어진 것은?

> · The book looks _____ .
> · I found the book _____ .

① interest – difficult
② interesting – difficult
③ interesting – difficulty
④ interestingly – difficult
⑤ interestingly – difficulty

10 두 문장의 뜻이 같도록 할 때 빈칸에 알맞은 것은?

> I asked her some questions.
> → I asked some questions _____ .

① her ② of her ③ to her
④ by her ⑤ for her

[11-12] 다음 중 문장의 형태가 나머지 넷과 다른 것을 고르시오.

11 ① I made him angry.
② My dad calls me Princess.
③ The lamp keeps the room bright.
④ They found the insect dangerous.
⑤ I gave her a present on her birthday.

12 ① Don't give me the trash.
② Can I ask you a question?
③ She bought her daughter a doll.
④ He told us some surprising news.
⑤ You should keep your hands clean.

서술형

[13-14] 어법상 틀린 부분을 찾아 바르게 고치시오.

13
> My new coat feels warm and softly.

_____ → _____

14
> I wrote a letter for my parents.

_____ → _____

서술형

[15-17] 우리말과 일치하도록 ( ) 안의 말을 이용하여 문장을 완성하시오.

15
> 레몬은 신맛이 난다. (sour)

→ Lemons _____ .

16
> 나는 그에게 내 공책을 빌려주었다.
> (lent, to, my notebook)

→ I _____ .

17
> 그 사고는 그녀를 불행하게 만들었다.
> (made, unhappy)

→ The accident _____ .

CHAPTER
05

The Passive
수동태

LET'S LOOK

The woman **helps** the old man.
The old man **is helped** by the woman.

수동태는 주어가 어떤 행위나 동작을 당할 때 사용하는 문장 형식이다.
'주어가 (～에 의해) ～되다'의 의미로 「be동사 + 과거분사」 형태로 나타낸다.

09 수동태 1
The Passive 1

1 능동태와 수동태

❶ 능동태

사람이나 사물이 '~하다'의 의미이다. 주어가 어떤 행위나 동작을 스스로 할 때 사용한다.

Everybody **loves** the girl.

The old man **fixes** the toys.

Many people **saw** the movie *Frozen*.

❷ 수동태

사람이나 사물이 '~되다'의 의미이다. 주어가 어떤 행위나 동작을 당할 때 사용한다.

The girl **is loved** by everybody.

The toys **are fixed** by the old man.

The movie *Frozen* **was seen** by many people.

2 수동태의 형태

❶ 수동태는 「be동사 + 과거분사」의 형태이며, 누구에 의해 일어난 일인지는 「by + 목적격」으로 나타낸다.

주어	be동사 + 과거분사	by + 목적격
My dog	is washed	by me.
The vegetables	are grown	by my parents.
The phone	was answered	by him.
The letters	were written	by Tony.

❷ 수동태의 부정문은 「be동사 + not + 과거분사」의 형태이다.

The milk **is not delivered** on Sundays.

The cookies **weren't eaten** by John.

LET'S CHECK

A   주어진 우리말에 알맞은 표현을 고르세요.

0	지어지다	☐ build	☑ be built
1	훔치다	☐ steal	☐ be stolen
2	초대받다	☐ invite	☐ be invited
3	만들다	☐ make	☐ be made
4	도움을 받다	☐ help	☐ be helped
5	배달하다	☐ deliver	☐ be delivered
6	재배되다	☐ grow	☐ be grown
7	읽다	☐ read	☐ be read
8	팔리다	☐ sell	☐ be sold
9	깨지다	☐ break	☐ be broken

B   ( ) 안에서 알맞은 말을 고르세요.

0   (1) Jack (washes, is washed) the car.

     (2) The car (washes, is washed) by Jack.

1   (1) My grandfather (made, was made) this bookcase.

     (2) This bookcase (made, was made) by my grandfather.

2   (1) Hangeul (created, was created) by King Sejong.

     (2) King Sejong (created, was created) Hangeul.

3   (1) Someone (stole, was stolen) my smart watch.

     (2) My smart watch (stole, was stolen) by someone.

4   (1) English (speaks, is spoken) in many countries.

     (2) People (speak, are spoken) English in many countries.

WORDS   B bookcase 책장, 책꽂이   create 창조하다

LET'S PRACTICE

A 주어진 문장이 능동태인지 수동태인지 고르세요.

		능동태	수동태
0	Harry ate noodles for lunch.	☑	☐
1	This movie was made in 1977.	☐	☐
2	The firemen put out the fire.	☐	☐
3	The ball was thrown by John.	☐	☐
4	Nancy was stung by a jellyfish.	☐	☐
5	The house was painted by my father.	☐	☐
6	I borrowed some books from the library.	☐	☐
7	This apartment building was built 25 years ago.	☐	☐
8	The teacher answered the students' questions.	☐	☐

B ( ) 안에서 알맞은 말을 고르세요.

0 The window (closed, (was closed)) by the teacher.

1 Lucy (read, was read) the novel in one day.

2 The thieves (hid, were hidden) the treasures in the cave.

3 Mike (bit, was bitten) by a dog.

4 My dad (took, was taken) these photos.

5 Laura (cleans, is cleaned) her desk every day.

6 The ring (found, was found) under the bed.

7 Susan (woke, was woken) up by the noise.

8 The letter (didn't write, wasn't written) by Sam.

9 They (don't grow, aren't grown) apples in their garden.

WORDS A noodles 국수 put out (불을) 끄다 sting 쏘다, 찌르다 jellyfish 해파리 borrow 빌리다 B novel 소설 thief 도둑 treasure 보물 cave 동굴 bite 물다 wake up (잠에서) 깨다, 깨우다

C 그림을 보고 ( ) 안에서 알맞은 말을 고르세요.

0	1	2	3

0 The vase (broke, (was broken)) by Tom.

1 The cat (chased, was chased) the mouse.

2 We (planted, were planted) a tree in our garden.

3 The soccer game (canceled, was canceled) yesterday.

D ( ) 안의 말을 알맞게 배열하여 문장을 완성하세요.

0 (is, rice, grown)

→ _____Rice is grown_____ by farmers.

1 (hotel, built, was, the)

→ _____ 100 years ago.

2 (was, fish, caught, the)

→ _____ by my brother.

3 (stolen, my, was, bike)

→ _____ yesterday.

4 (are, shoes, made, not)

→ _____ in that factory.

WORDS   C chase 뒤쫓다 plant 심다 cancel 취소하다   D rice 쌀 catch 잡다 factory 공장

10 수동태 2
The Passive 2

1 수동태 문장 전환

❶ 능동태의 목적어가 수동태의 주어가 된다.

❷ 능동태의 동사는 「be동사 + 과거분사」로 바꾼다.

❸ 능동태의 주어는 「by + 목적격」으로 바꾼다.

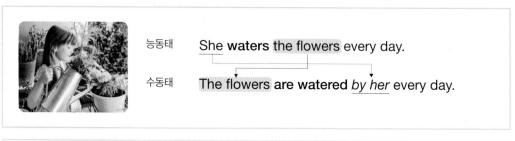

능동태	She **waters** the flowers every day.
수동태	The flowers **are watered** *by her* every day.

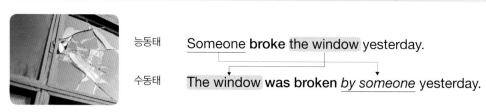

능동태	Someone **broke** the window yesterday.
수동태	The window **was broken** *by someone* yesterday.

2 「by + 목적격」의 생략

수동태에서 행위자가 일반적인 사람들이거나 중요하지 않을 경우 생략할 수 있다.

Snails **are eaten** (by people) in France.

The bank **was robbed** (by someone) yesterday.

> **✎ NOTE** 행위자가 중요한 경우 「by + 목적격」은 생략하지 않는다.
> The Mona Lisa **was painted** *by Leonardo da Vinci*.

LET'S CHECK

A 다음 현재형 문장을 수동태로 바꿔 쓰세요.

0 She cleans the table.

→ The table _____is_____ _____cleaned_____ by her.

1 We use the computers.

→ The computers _____ _____ by us.

2 Many people love pizza.

→ Pizza _____ _____ by many people.

3 Mr. Green teaches the math class.

→ The math class _____ _____ by Mr. Green.

4 They sell fresh vegetables at the market.

→ Fresh vegetables _____ _____ at the market.

B 다음 과거형 문장을 수동태로 바꿔 쓰세요.

0 David solved the problem.

→ The problem _____was_____ _____solved_____ by David.

1 Linda played the piano.

→ The piano _____ _____ by Linda.

2 Someone painted the office last week.

→ The office _____ _____ last week.

3 The storm destroyed the houses.

→ The houses _____ _____ by the storm.

4 Shakespeare wrote *Hamlet*.

→ *Hamlet* _____ _____ by Shakespeare.

WORDS B solve 풀다, 해결하다 storm 폭풍, 폭풍우 destroy 파괴하다

LET'S PRACTICE

A 그림을 보고 보기에서 알맞은 말을 골라 수동태 문장을 완성하세요. (현재형으로 쓸 것)

| 보기 | ~~collect~~ | park | serve | wash |

0 The trash ___is collected___ every Wednesday.

1 Breakfast _____ between 7:00 and 9:00.

2 Two cars _____ in the garage.

3 The dishes _____ by Jean every day.

B ( ) 안의 말을 이용하여 수동태 문장을 완성하세요. (현재형 또는 과거형으로 쓸 것)

0 Paper ___is made___ from wood. (make)

1 Pyramids _____ by Egyptians. (build)

2 Many trees _____ every year. (cut)

3 The door _____ last week. (paint)

4 Spanish _____ in many countries. (speak)

5 George _____ by a soccer ball. (hit)

6 The light bulb _____ by Thomas Edison. (invent)

7 The missing child _____ at the mall. (find)

8 The dog _____ by him every day. (walk)

9 The flowers _____ by John yesterday. (send)

WORDS A serve 제공하다 park 주차하다 trash 쓰레기 garage 차고 B Egyptian 이집트 사람 light bulb 전구 missing 없어진, 실종된

C

주어진 문장을 수동태로 바꿔 쓰세요.

0 Cathy buys the books.

→ _The books are bought by Cathy._

1 The manager closes the shop.

→ _____

2 Robert changed the flat tire.

→ _____

3 Many people saw the accident.

→ _____

4 The teacher corrected the mistakes.

→ _____

D

밑줄 친 부분을 바르게 고치세요.

0 The classroom <u>cleans</u> every day.   →   _is cleaned_

1 Mary <u>was invited</u> me to her party.   →

2 The guests <u>were enjoyed</u> the dinner.   →

3 My backpack <u>stole</u> last night.   →

4 They <u>are grown</u> corns and peas.   →

5 Luke <u>was broken</u> his leg last week.   →

6 My sandwich <u>ate</u> by my dog.   →

7 Gaudi <u>was designed</u> this building.   →

8 The tablet PC was fixed <u>by he</u>.   →

9 The phone bill <u>didn't pay</u> last month.   →

WORDS C flat tire 바람 빠진 타이어 accident 사고 correct 맞는, 옳은; *고치다 D corn 옥수수 pea 완두콩 phone bill 전화 요금 pay 지불하다

빈칸 완성 ( ) 안의 말을 이용하여 문장을 완성하세요.

1 나의 새 자전거는 도난 당했다. (steal)

→ My new bike _____ _____ .

2 이 방은 우리 부모님이 사용하신다. (use)

→ This room _____ _____ by my parents.

3 신발은 2층에서 판매된다. (sell)

→ Shoes _____ _____ on the second floor.

4 이 개집은 우리 아빠가 지었다. (build)

→ This doghouse _____ _____ by my dad.

5 많은 차들이 길을 따라 주차되어 있었다. (park)

→ Many cars _____ _____ along the street.

어구 배열 우리말과 일치하도록 ( ) 안의 말을 알맞게 배열하세요.

6 Sam은 벌에게 쏘였다. (was, a, Sam, by, stung, bee)

→ _____

7 그 이메일은 Kevin이 썼다. (the, by, written, Kevin, was, email)

→ _____

8 솜사탕은 설탕으로 만들어진다. (cotton candy, made, is, sugar, of)

→ _____

9 이 책은 1997년에 출판되었다. (1997, published, this, was, book, in)

→ _____

10 그 배우는 많은 사람들에게 사랑을 받는다. (is, the, many, loved, peoples, actor, by)

→ _____

STEP 3 영작하기 ( ) 안의 말을 이용하여 우리말을 영어로 옮기세요.

11 크리켓은 영국에서 경기된다. (Cricket, play, in England)

→ _____

12 개구리는 뱀에게 먹힌다. (frogs, eat, snakes)

→ _____

13 그 자물쇠는 누군가에 의해 부서졌다. (the lock, broke, someone)

→ _____

14 그 건물은 이탈리아 사람에 의해 설계되었다. (the building, design, an Italian)

→ _____

15 영어와 프랑스어는 캐나다에서 쓰인다. (English and French, speak, in Canada)

→ _____

16 우리는 Helen의 결혼식에 초대되었다. (invite, to Helen's wedding)

→ _____

17 그 병들은 선반 위에 놓여있다. (the bottles, place, on the shelf)

→ _____

18 100명이 비행기 추락 사고로 죽었다. (a hundred people, kill, in the plane crash)

→ _____

19 내 컴퓨터는 지난주 월요일에 배달되었다. (my computer, deliver, last Monday)

→ _____

20 그 장미들은 나의 할머니가 심으셨다. (the roses, plant, my grandmother)

→ _____

1 빈칸에 들어갈 말로 알맞은 것은?

> The dinner table _____ in the garden.

① set
② sets
③ was set
④ were set
⑤ is setting

2 빈칸에 들어갈 말로 알맞지 <u>않은</u> 것은?

> The story was written by _____.

① me
② her
③ us
④ they
⑤ my sister

[3-4] 다음 우리말을 영어로 바르게 옮긴 것을 고르시오.

3

> 이 그림은 내 여동생이 그렸다.

① My sister is painted this picture.
② My sister painted by this picture.
③ My sister was painted this picture.
④ This picture did painted by my sister.
⑤ This picture was painted by my sister.

4

> 그녀는 Tom의 초대를 받지 않았다.

① She didn't invite Tom.
② She wasn't invited Tom.
③ She wasn't invite by Tom.
④ She didn't invited by Tom.
⑤ She wasn't invited by Tom.

5 다음 문장을 수동태로 바꿀 때 밑줄 친 부분을 생략할 수 <u>없는</u> 것은?

① <u>We</u> keep books in a bookcase.
② <u>People</u> speak French in Kenya.
③ <u>They</u> serve dinner at six o'clock.
④ <u>Mr. Kim</u> helped the new student.
⑤ <u>Someone</u> found my wallet yesterday.

6 우리말과 일치하도록 ( ) 안의 말을 알맞게 배열하시오.

> 그 잡지는 많은 여성들에게 읽힌다.
> (read, by, is, magazine, many, the, women)

→ _____

[7-8] 밑줄 친 부분이 <u>잘못된</u> 것을 고르시오.

7
① The cat <u>is fed</u> by me.
② The song <u>is sung</u> by Julie.
③ The boxes <u>are carried</u> by him.
④ The bus <u>is driven</u> by my uncle.
⑤ The man <u>was stolen</u> the gold ring.

8
① The cars <u>are made</u> in Japan.
② The radio <u>was invented</u> in 1896.
③ Mr. Brown <u>teaches</u> the math class.
④ The game <u>watched</u> by many people.
⑤ Peter <u>made</u> Korean dishes yesterday.

9 다음 중 어법상 옳은 문장은?

① The puzzle finished by Paul.
② The food bought by my mom.
③ Everyone was enjoyed the party.
④ The speech was given by Dr. Philip.
⑤ A famous chef was made this pasta.

10 빈칸에 들어갈 말이 순서대로 바르게 짝지어진 것은?

· Emma _____ the laundry.
· The laundry _____ by Emma.

① did – done
② did – was did
③ did – was done
④ was done – did
⑤ was done – done

11 다음 중 수동태로 바꾼 것이 옳지 <u>않은</u> 것은?

① A car hit my friend.
  → My friend was hit by a car.
② Susan made the donuts.
  → The donuts are made by Susan.
③ They clean the streets every day.
  → The streets are cleaned every day.
④ Tim changed the light bulb.
  → The light bulb was changed by Tim.
⑤ The dealer sold two cars yesterday.
  → Two cars were sold by the dealer yesterday.

서술형

[12-13] 다음 문장을 수동태로 바꿔 쓸 때 빈칸에 알맞은 말을 쓰시오.

12

They grow coffee in Brazil.

→ Coffee _____ in Brazil.

13

The worker fixed the door.

→ The door _____ by the worker.

서술형

[14-16] 우리말과 일치하도록 ( ) 안의 말을 이용하여 문장을 완성하시오.

14

네덜란드어는 네덜란드에서 사용된다. (speak)

→ Dutch _____ in the Netherlands.

15

이 웨딩드레스는 우리 엄마가 입었던 것이다. (wear)

→ This wedding dress _____ by my mom.

16

그 쿠키들은 John이 먹었다. (eat)

→ The cookies _____ by John.

CHAPTER
06

Conjunctions
접속사

LET'S LOOK

An elephant is large **and** strong.

He woke up
when the alarm clock rang.

접속사는 단어와 단어, 구와 구, 절과 절을 연결하는 말이다. **and, but, or, so**는
두 개 이상의 말을 대등하게 연결하고, **when, while, before, after, because, if**는
부사절을 이끌어 절과 절을 연결한다.

11

접속사 1
Conjunctions 1

and, but, or, so는 단어와 단어, 구와 구, 절과 절 등을 하나로 연결한다. 문법적으로 대등한 것을 연결하기 때문에 등위 접속사라고 한다.

1

and: ~와/과, 그리고

내용상 서로 비슷한 것을 연결한다.

The girl is *young* **and** *beautiful*.

I bought *red socks* **and** *white sneakers*.

My parents love me, **and** *I love them, too.*

> **✎NOTE** 셋 이상을 연결할 때는 A, B, and C의 형태로 쓴다.
>
> I like *apples*, *bananas*, **and** *oranges*. [○]
>
> I like *apples* **and** *bananas* **and** *oranges*. [×]

2

but: 하지만, 그러나

내용상 서로 반대인 것을 연결한다.

The weather was *sunny* **but** *cold*.

It *smelled delicious* **but** *tasted terrible*.

Penguins have wings, **but** *they can't fly*.

3

or: 또는, ~거나

둘 이상의 선택해야 할 것을 연결한다.

Is the answer *right* **or** *wrong*?

We can get there *by bus* **or** *on foot*.

Did you call Jake, **or** *did Jake call you?*

4

so: 그래서, 그러므로

절과 절을 연결하며 앞 뒤 절이 원인과 결과를 나타낸다. so 앞에는 콤마(,)를 쓴다.

The room was dark, **so** *he turned on the light*.

I want to be healthy, **so** *I exercise regularly*.

LET'S CHECK

A ( ) 안에서 알맞은 말을 고르세요.

0   Bees ((and) or) butterflies are insects.

1   The king was rich (and, but) unhappy.

2   David walks (but, or) bikes to school.

3   Jane is a good singer, (but, so) I'm not.

4   He talked, (and, or) I listened.

5   I can't play the piano, (and, but) she can.

6   It will rain (but, or) snow tomorrow.

7   Sam lived in France, (but, so) he can speak French.

8   Linda is tall, (but, so) her sisters are short.

9   There are spoons, forks, (and, but) knives on the table.

B 자연스러운 문장이 되도록 알맞게 연결하세요.

0   There are a dog and •   • ⓐ leave the room.

1   It's spring but   •   • ⓑ still cold.

2   Please be quiet or   •   • ⓒ watching TV?

3   It was late, so   •   • ⓓ I didn't get wet.

4   Peter can swim and   •   • ⓔ play tennis.

5   Is she studying or   •   • ⓕ her puppies.

6   I had an umbrella, so   •   • ⓖ we took a taxi.

WORDS   A insect 곤충   unhappy 불행한   short 짧은: *키가 작은   knife 칼   B get wet 젖다

LET'S PRACTICE

A 빈칸에 and, but, or, so 중 알맞은 접속사를 넣어 문장을 완성하세요.

0 My brother is tall _____and_____ slim.

1 I am tired, _____ I will go to bed early.

2 I love soccer, _____ I don't like baseball.

3 Is that man your father _____ your uncle?

4 The war started in 1939 _____ ended in 1945.

5 The dress was very nice _____ expensive.

6 Will you use this chair, _____ can I use it?

7 The boy was hungry, _____ he ate the cookies.

8 I need milk, fruit, _____ ice to make a smoothie.

9 The keys may be on the table _____ in that drawer.

B 그림을 보고 보기에서 알맞은 말을 골라 문장을 완성하세요. (단, 한 번씩만 쓸 것)

0	1	2	3

보기	~~and~~	but	or	so

0 David is wearing a T-shirt _____and_____ shorts.

1 Who's taller? Mike _____ Bill?

2 It was cold, _____ we stayed at home.

3 She washed her jeans, _____ they didn't get clean.

WORDS A slim 날씬한 war 전쟁 end 끝나다 smoothie 스무디 drawer 서랍   B shorts 반바지 get clean 깨끗해지다

C ( ) 안의 말을 이용하여 두 문장을 한 문장으로 만드세요.

0 Jane put milk in her tea. She put sugar in her tea. (and)

→ _____ Jane put milk and sugar in her tea. _____

1 Is that a duck? Is it a goose? (or)

→ _____

2 The ship carries people. It carries things. (and)

→ _____

3 Tom did his best. He failed the exam. (but)

→ _____

4 It was dusty outside. I closed the window. (so)

→ _____

D 밑줄 친 부분을 바르게 고치세요.

0 My mom <u>or</u> dad go hiking together.   →   and

1 Is the baby a boy <u>and</u> a girl?   →

2 He was so tired, <u>or</u> he took a nap.   →

3 She sat down <u>but</u> read a magazine.   →

4 Is it Wednesday <u>and</u> Thursday?   →

5 The coat was cheap, <u>or</u> I bought it.   →

6 He can speak Korean, <u>so</u> his wife can't.   →

7 The roller coaster was scary <u>and</u> fun.   →

8 They weren't busy, <u>but</u> they helped me.   →

9 Will you save the money <u>so</u> spend it?   →

WORDS C goose 거위 carry 운반하다 fail 실패하다, (시험에) 떨어지다 dusty 먼지가 많은 D cheap 값이 싼 scary 무서운 save 저축하다 spend (돈을) 쓰다

UNIT 12 접속사 2
Conjunctions 2

when, while, before, after, because, if는 시간, 이유, 조건의 의미를 나타내는 접속사로, 절과 절을 연결한다. 이때, 이 접속사들이 이끄는 절을 부사절, 나머지 절을 주절이라고 한다.

1 when: ～할 때

I listen to music **when** *I have free time*.
Helen lived in Busan **when** *she was young*.
When *the phone rang*, Kevin was sleeping.

2 while: ～하는 동안

I met my friend **while** *I was waiting for a bus*.
They visited Rome **while** *they were in Italy*.
While *I was washing the dishes*, Bill was cleaning the house.

3 before: ～하기 전에 / after: ～한 후에

Before *you go to bed*, brush your teeth.
Judy went home **after** *she finished shopping*.

4 because: ～때문에

We didn't swim **because** *the water wasn't clean*.
(= The water wasn't clean, **so** we didn't swim.)

5 if: 만약 ～하다면

If *it rains*, we will cancel our trip.

> **NOTE** 1. 시간과 조건의 부사절에서 쓰인 동사는 미래형 대신 현재형을 쓴다.
> I will go out **after** I *finish* my homework.
> **If** you *rest*, you will feel better.
>
> 2. 부사절이 주절 앞에 올 경우에는 부사절 끝에 콤마(,)를 쓴다.
> **When** *I have a cold*, I drink lemon tea.
>   부사절   주절

LET'S CHECK

A 보기에서 알맞은 말을 골라 문장을 완성하세요. (단, 한 번씩만 쓸 것)

보기	~~when~~	while	before	after	because	if

0   She started to play the piano _____ when _____ she was seven.

1   It rained _____ the kids were playing in the garden.

2   Mike had breakfast _____ he got up.

3   I left early _____ I didn't want to miss the bus.

4   _____ you give the correct answer, you will get a prize.

5   _____ they bought the house, they lived in an apartment.

B 자연스러운 문장이 되도록 알맞게 연결하세요.

0   Susan was unhappy   •   • ⓐ before you ask a question.

1   I'll visit you   •   • ⓑ because he isn't honest.

2   My headache stopped   •   • ⓒ if I'm not busy.

3   Raise your hand   •   • ⓓ we will visit Opera House.

4   Sue cut her finger   •   • ⓔ because her dog was sick.

5   I don't like him   •   • ⓕ while she was cooking.

6   If we go to Sydney,   •   • ⓖ after I took the medicine.

WORDS   **A** prize 상   **B** headache 두통   raise 들다, 올리다   finger 손가락   honest 정직한   medicine 약

LET'S PRACTICE

A 앞 문장에 이어질 말로 자연스러운 것을 고르세요.

0   I love kittens

☐ when I was little.

☑ because they are so cute.

1   If it snows tomorrow,

☐ we had a snowball fight.

☐ I'll make a snowman.

2   The boy was crying

☐ when I found him.

☐ because he wasn't hungry.

3   Don't use your cellphone

☐ while you are driving.

☐ before you get in the car.

4   She opened the windows

☐ if it is too cold.

☐ because it was sunny.

B ( ) 안에서 알맞은 말을 고르세요.

0   I can share my lunch (if, before) you are hungry.

1   The fire alarm rang (while, if) we were taking a test.

2   I like her (after, because) she is kind to me.

3   (If, After) you are tired, you can go home now.

4   It was 12 o'clock (when, because) he woke up.

5   She went to bed (before, after) she took a shower.

6   I must go to the supermarket (before, after) it closes.

7   I lost my wallet (while, If) I was riding my bike.

8   You can drive a car when you (are, will be) older.

9   If you (don't, won't) water the plants, they will die.

WORDS A kitten 새끼 고양이   little 작은; *어린   snowball fight 눈싸움   snowman 눈사람   get in the car 차에 타다   B share 나누다, 함께 쓰다   fire alarm 화재 경보기   die 죽다

C 그림을 보고 보기에서 알맞은 말을 골라 문장을 완성하세요. (단, 한 번씩만 쓸 것)

0  1  2  3

보기   while   before   because   if

0   Sally fell on the ice_____while_____ she was ice-skating.

1   _____ it rains, I will wear my new raincoat.

2   Look both ways _____ you cross the street.

3   Tom didn't go to school _____ he was sick.

D 주어진 접속사를 이용하여 두 문장을 한 문장으로 만드세요.

0   The boy ran away. He broke the window.
    → _____The boy ran away_____ after _____he broke the window_____ .

1   You can use my phone. You need it.
    → _____ when _____ .

2   Peter fell asleep. He was reading.
    → _____ while _____ .

3   I was thirsty. I drank a glass of water.
    → _____ because _____ .

4   You run. You will catch the bus.
    → _____ if _____ .

WORDS   C raincoat 우비 both ways 양쪽 cross 건너다   D fall asleep 잠들다 thirsty 목마른

STEP 1

빈칸 완성 보기에서 알맞은 말을 골라 문장을 완성하세요.

보기	and	or	if	because	when

1 그는 과일 샐러드와 샌드위치를 주문했다.

   → He ordered a fruit salad   a sandwich.

2 사자와 치타 중 어느 것이 빠릅니까?

   → Which is faster, a lion   a cheetah?

3 신호가 초록색일 때 길을 건너라.

   → Cross the street   the traffic light is green.

4 나는 음악 소리가 너무 커서 잠에서 깼다.

   → I woke up   the music was too loud.

5 오른쪽으로 돌면, 너는 은행을 발견할 것이다.

   →   you turn right, you will find a bank.

STEP 2

어구 배열 우리말과 일치하도록 ( ) 안의 말을 알맞게 배열하세요.

6 Sally는 노래하고 춤을 출 수 있다. (can, Sally, sing, dance, and)

   → _____

7 그녀는 어리지만 현명하다. (wise, young, she, but, is)

   → _____

8 우리는 아빠가 집에 오신 후에 저녁을 먹었다. (ate, home, after, Dad, dinner, came)

   → We _____.

9 커피를 드시겠어요, 차를 드시겠어요? (you, or, tea, have, coffee, will)

   → _____

10 어두워지기 전에 집에 가자. (it, before, gets, home, dark, go)

   → Let's _____.

영작하기 ( ) 안의 말을 이용하여 우리말을 영어로 옮기세요.

11 Tom은 그 도시를 떠나 뉴욕으로 이사갔다. (move to, New York)

→ Tom left the city _____ .

12 비가 내리고 있었지만, 춥지는 않았다. (it, cold)

→ It was raining, _____ .

13 너는 칼이나 가위 있니? (a knife, scissors)

→ Do you have _____ ?

14 전화기가 울렸을 때, 나는 자고 있었다. (the phone, ring)

→ _____ , I was sleeping.

15 나는 공부를 하는 동안 음악을 듣는다. (study)

→ I listen to music _____ .

16 그는 들어오기 전에 신발을 벗었다. (come in)

→ He took off his shoes _____ .

17 그는 일어나서, 라디오를 켰다. (wake up)

→ _____ , he turned on the radio.

18 네가 공부를 열심히 하면 시험에 합격할 것이다. (study, hard)

→ You will pass the exam _____ .

19 그는 캐나다에 살아서 영어를 잘 말할 수 있다. (can, speak, English, well)

→ He lives in Canada, _____ .

20 우리는 친구니까 내가 널 도와줄게. (friends)

→ _____ , I'll help you.

REVIEW TEST
CHAPTER 06

[1-4] 빈칸에 들어갈 말로 알맞은 것을 고르시오.

1

My name is Hyorin, _____ my sister's name is Jimin.

① if   ② or   ③ so
④ and   ⑤ when

2

I don't like the movie _____ it is too violent.

① and   ② but   ③ so
④ while   ⑤ because

3

Dinner was ready _____ he came home.

① if   ② or   ③ but
④ when   ⑤ because

4

We will go to the zoo _____ it is sunny tomorrow.

① if   ② or   ③ but
④ and   ⑤ because

서술형

5 빈칸에 공통으로 들어갈 접속사를 쓰시오.

· He feels lonely _____ he has few friends.
· I like summer _____ I can swim in the sea.

서술형

[6-7] 두 문장의 뜻이 같도록 할 때 빈칸에 알맞은 접속사를 쓰시오.

6

At the age of 13, he started to play the guitar.

→ _____ he was 13 years old, he started to play the guitar.

7

He turned off the TV, and then he left the room.

→ _____ he left the room, he turned off the TV.

8 빈칸에 들어갈 접속사가 나머지 넷과 다른 것은?

① Penguins _____ ducks are birds.
② I need a stamp _____ an envelope.
③ He can speak English _____ French.
④ Is a tomato a fruit _____ a vegetable?
⑤ She washed her face _____ her hands.

9 다음 중 어법상 옳지 <u>않은</u> 문장은?

① When I grow up, I will be a designer.

② If we will work together, we can do it.

③ Ann is popular because she sings well.

④ After I clean the house, I will watch TV.

⑤ She washed the apple before she ate it.

[10-11] 빈칸에 들어갈 말이 순서대로 바르게 짝지어진 것을 고르시오.

10

· Mr. Moon _____ Mrs. Song are a couple.

· We can go out for dinner now _____ later.

① or – or   ② or – but

③ and – or   ④ and – so

⑤ but – and

11

· We went by bus _____ it was cheap.

· You can get a seat _____ you come early.

① if – so   ② if – when

③ if – because   ④ because – if

⑤ because – so

12 밑줄 친 부분의 쓰임이 나머지 넷과 <u>다른</u> 것은?

① I wear my gloves <u>when</u> it is cold.

② She cried <u>when</u> she fell off the bike.

③ <u>When</u> will you finish your homework?

④ <u>When</u> you come back, I won't be here.

⑤ He became an actor <u>when</u> he was twelve.

서술형

[13-14] 우리말과 일치하도록 밑줄 친 부분을 바르게 고치시오.

13

나는 동물을 좋아하기 때문에 수의사가 될 것이다.

→ <u>If</u> I like animals, I will be a vet.

→ _____

14

그는 모든 것을 가졌지만, 행복하지 않았다.

→ He had everything, <u>so</u> he wasn't happy.

→ _____

서술형

[15-17] 우리말과 일치하도록 ( ) 안의 말을 이용하여 문장을 완성하시오.

15

그 책은 흥미롭고 유용하다. (interesting, useful)

→ The book is

_____ .

16

그들은 식사를 하는 동안 말하지 않는다. (eat)

→ They don't speak

_____ .

17

비가 오면, 우리는 집에 머물 것이다. (it, rain)

→ _____ ,

we will stay at home.

CHAPTER
07

Relative Pronouns
관계대명사

LET'S LOOK

A doctor is a person
who treats sick people.

These are cookies
which my mom made.

관계대명사는 앞에 오는 명사를 꾸며주는 **형용사절**을 이끄는 말이다. who(m), which, that 등이 있으며, 형용사절에서 하는 역할에 따라 **주격**, **목적격** 등으로 나뉜다.

13

관계대명사 1
Relative Pronouns 1

1 관계대명사의 쓰임

❶ 형용사절을 이끌어 앞에 오는 명사(선행사)를 꾸며준다.

a girl **who** lives next door 옆집에 사는 소녀

a jacket **which** I bought 내가 산 재킷

> **NOTE** 명사를 앞에서 꾸미는 형용사와는 달리, 형용사절은 명사를 뒤에서 꾸며준다.
>
> a pretty *girl* 예쁜 소녀   *a girl* who won the race 경주에서 우승한 소녀

❷ 접속사와 대명사 역할을 동시에 한다.

I met *a man*. + **He** is a famous writer.

→ I met *a man* **who** is a famous writer.
  (who = He를 대신함)

I ate *the cake*. + My mom made **it**.

→ I ate *the cake* **which** my mom made.
  (which = it을 대신함)

2 관계대명사의 종류

❶ 사람에 대해 설명할 때는 who를 쓴다.

I know *a boy* **who** has a nice smile.

I like *the people* **who** live next door.

❷ 사물, 동물에 대해 설명할 때는 which를 쓴다.

Ice cream is *a dessert* **which** children love.

A pony is *a horse* **which** is very small.

❸ that은 종류에 관계없이 모두 쓸 수 있다.

Susan is *the girl* **that** is wearing the pink coat.

These are *photos* **that** we took in Hawaii.

LET'S CHECK

A 형용사절에는 밑줄을 치고, 형용사절이 꾸미는 말에는 동그라미 하세요.

0   I met (a woman) who is 99 years old.

1   A thief is a person who steals things.

2   He lives in a house that has a pool.

3   I ate the noodles which my mom made.

4   John is the boy who is riding the bike.

5   This is the movie that I watched last night.

6   The patient pointed at the tooth that hurt.

7   Terry is wearing socks which have holes.

8   Is there a shop which sells fruit?

9   Is that the policeman who helped you?

B 우리말과 일치하도록 알맞게 연결하세요.

0   (1) 그녀가 읽었던 책 •   • ⓐ the book which reads well

    (2) 잘 읽히는 책 •   • ⓑ the book which she read

1   (1) 나를 좋아하는 소녀 •   • ⓐ the girl who I like

    (2) 내가 좋아하는 소녀 •   • ⓑ the girl who likes me

2   (1) 그녀가 산 가방 •   • ⓐ the bag which she bought

    (2) 비싸 보이는 가방 •   • ⓑ the bag which looks expensive

3   (1) 작년에 지어진 집 •   • ⓐ the house which my dad built

    (2) 우리 아빠가 지은 집 •   • ⓑ the house which was built last year

4   (1) 나를 도와준 남자 •   • ⓐ the man who helped me

    (2) 내가 도와준 남자 •   • ⓑ the man who I helped

WORDS   A patient 환자   point 가리키다   tooth 이, 치아   hurt 아프다   hole 구멍   B read 읽다; *읽히다

3 주격 관계대명사

형용사절에서 주어 역할을 하는 관계대명사이다. 주격 관계대명사는 설명하는 말이 사람일 때 who, 사물, 동물일 때 which를 쓴다. that은 종류에 관계없이 모두 쓸 수 있다.

I like *people*. + **They** are kind and friendly.

→ I like *people* **who** are kind and friendly.
  I like *people* **that** are kind and friendly.

The picture is interesting. + **It** is on the wall.

→ *The picture* **which** is on the wall is interesting.
  The picture **that** is on the wall is interesting.

✎ NOTE 형용사절은 수식하는 명사(선행사) 바로 뒤에 와야 한다.
  The steak was delicious **which** we ate at the restaurant. [×]
  The steak **which** we ate at the restaurant was delicious. [○]

4 주격 관계대명사의 수 일치

주격 관계대명사가 이끄는 형용사절의 동사는 반드시 선행사의 수와 일치해야 한다.

I have *a cousin* **who** *lives* in Boston.
└── (단수) ──┘

I have *cousins* **who** *live* in Boston.
└── (복수) ──┘

LET'S CHECK

C   빈칸에 who 또는 which를 넣어 문장을 완성하세요.

0   He wants a house _____which_____ has three bedrooms.

1   The boy _____ came here yesterday is John.

2   This is the man _____ found our dog.

3   We stayed at a hotel _____ is near the park.

4   Emily has a machine _____ makes waffles.

5   What is the name of the girl _____ is sitting on the bench?

6   The student _____ failed the test cried.

7   Where is the money _____ was on the desk?

8   I know some people _____ live in Japan.

9   Stella has a cat _____ has black fur.

D   ( ) 안에서 알맞은 말을 고르세요.

0   I have a friend who (is, are) a great singer.

1   Peter has some friends who (is, are) from Australia.

2   The man who (live, lives) next door is a dentist.

3   Students who (study, studies) hard will get good grades.

4   Did you see the keys which (was, were) next to the TV?

5   My dad works for a company that (make, makes) batteries.

6   The girl who (is, are) talking to Philip is my sister.

7   The woman who (sell, sells) flowers is kind.

8   Is there a restaurant that (open, opens) before 8:00 a.m.?

9   Tony is wearing boots which (is, are) wet and muddy.

WORDS   C near ~ 근처에, 가까이에   fur 털   D grade 성적   battery 건전지, 배터리   muddy 진흙투성이인

LET'S PRACTICE

A 밑줄 친 부분을 who 또는 which로 바꿔 쓰세요.

0	I called my friend <u>that</u> lives in Canada.	→	who
1	The apples <u>that</u> are on the table are fresh.	→	
2	A baker is a person <u>that</u> makes cakes and bread.	→	
3	The children <u>that</u> are playing outside look happy.	→	
4	He lives in a house <u>that</u> isn't very big.	→	
5	The man <u>that</u> works in the shop is polite.	→	
6	Kelly always wears skirts <u>that</u> are too short.	→	
7	Kevin lost his jacket <u>that</u> was expensive.	→	
8	The kids <u>that</u> live upstairs are noisy.	→	
9	The dog <u>that</u> bit me ran away.	→	

B 빈칸에 들어갈 말로 알맞은 것을 고르세요.

0 Brian has a camera which _____ new.

ⓐ am   ⓑ are   ✓ⓒ is

1 The man who _____ in the kitchen is my father.

ⓐ am   ⓑ are   ⓒ is

2 The books which _____ on the table are mine.

ⓐ am   ⓑ are   ⓒ is

3 I met a girl who _____ the same name as me.

ⓐ has   ⓑ have   ⓒ having

4 The elephants which _____ in Africa are big.

ⓐ live   ⓑ lives   ⓒ living

WORDS A baker 제빵사 polite 예의 바른, 공손한 upstairs 위층에 noisy 시끄러운

C 그림을 보고 보기에서 알맞은 말을 골라 who 또는 which와 함께 써서 문장을 완성하세요.

0 1 2 3

보기	clean floors automatically	~~fly an airplane~~
	treat sick animals	wash dirty dishes

0　A pilot is a person ＿＿＿*who flies an airplane*＿＿＿ .

1　A dishwasher is a machine ＿＿＿＿＿＿＿＿＿＿ .

2　A vet is a person ＿＿＿＿＿＿＿＿＿＿ .

3　A robot vacuum cleaner is a machine ＿＿＿＿＿＿＿＿＿＿ .

D 관계대명사를 이용하여 두 문장을 한 문장으로 만드세요. (who 또는 which를 사용할 것)

0　I know a boy. He speaks English well.

→ I know a boy ＿＿＿*who speaks English well*＿＿＿ .

1　A camel is an animal. It lives in the desert.

→ A camel is an animal ＿＿＿＿＿＿＿＿＿＿ .

2　Tom bought pants. They didn't fit him well.

→ Tom bought pants ＿＿＿＿＿＿＿＿＿＿ .

3　The man was my brother. He called me.

→ The man ＿＿＿＿＿＿＿＿＿＿ was my brother.

4　We went to a restaurant. It is near the hotel.

→ We went to a restaurant ＿＿＿＿＿＿＿＿＿＿ .

WORDS　C automatically 자동으로　fly 날다; *조종하다　treat 치료하다　vet 수의사　D camel 낙타　desert 사막　fit 맞다

14 관계대명사 2
Relative Pronouns 2

1 ### 목적격 관계대명사

형용사절에서 목적어 역할을 하는 관계대명사이다. 목적격 관계대명사는 설명하는 말이 사람일 때 who(m), 사물, 동물일 때 which를 쓴다. that은 종류에 관계없이 모두 쓸 수 있다.

He is *the man*. I saw **the man** on TV last night.

↓

→ He is *the man* <u>who(m)</u> I saw on TV last night.
He is *the man* <u>that</u> I saw on TV last night.

The sweater is warm. I bought **it** yesterday.

↓

→ The sweater <u>which</u> I bought yesterday is warm.
The sweater <u>that</u> I bought yesterday is warm.

✏NOTE 형용사절에서 목적격 관계대명사가 대신하는 목적어를 중복해서 쓰지 않도록 주의한다.
He is *the man* **who(m)** I saw ~~the man~~ on TV last night. [×]
The sweater **which** I bought ~~it~~ yesterday is warm. [×]

+PLUS 일상회화에서는 주로 whom 대신 who를 쓴다.

2 ### 목적격 관계대명사의 생략

목적격 관계대명사는 생략할 수 있다. 선행사(명사) 뒤에 「주어 + 동사」가 나오면 목적격 관계대명사가 생략되었다고 볼 수 있다.

The woman <u>we met</u> at the mall is my teacher.
= who(m)[that] we met at the mall

The cookies <u>you made</u> were delicious.
= which[that] you made

✏NOTE 주격 관계대명사는 생략할 수 없다.
The man **who** wrote this novel is young. [○]
The man **wrote** this novel is young. [×]

LET'S CHECK

A 밑줄 친 관계대명사가 주격인지 목적격인지 고르세요.

		주격	목적격
0	Mr. Roberts is a teacher <u>who</u> I like very much.	☐	☑
1	Mr. Roberts is a teacher <u>who</u> teaches us math.	☐	☐
2	Florence is a city <u>which</u> is in Italy.	☐	☐
3	Florence is a city <u>which</u> I visited last summer.	☐	☐
4	The man <u>that</u> wrote this letter is my uncle.	☐	☐
5	The man <u>that</u> you saw yesterday is my uncle.	☐	☐
6	Linda is reading a book <u>that</u> I lent to her.	☐	☐
7	Linda is reading a book <u>that</u> has a lot of pictures.	☐	☐

B 주어진 문장에서 목적격 관계대명사가 생략된 곳에 ✓로 표시하세요.

0   The dog ✓ Dylan has is smart.

1   The actor we met is not famous.

2   These are shoes I usually wear.

3   Brian is a person everybody likes.

4   The bus we took this morning was empty.

5   The dress you're wearing is nice.

6   The man I called didn't answer the phone.

7   All the guests Amy invited came to the party.

8   I liked the museum we visited last weekend.

9   My mom liked my friend I brought home yesterday.

WORDS   A Florence 플로렌스 (이탈리아 중부의 도시, 피렌체)   B bring 가져오다; *데려오다

LET'S PRACTICE

A 빈칸에 들어갈 수 있는 관계대명사를 모두 고르세요.

0 The people _____ I met yesterday were kind.

 ⓐ who   ⓑ whom   ⓒ which   ✓ⓓ that

1 The tomatoes _____ my mom grows are fresh.

 ⓐ who   ⓑ whom   ⓒ which   ⓓ that

2 Grandma is the person _____ I like the most.

 ⓐ who   ⓑ whom   ⓒ which   ⓓ that

3 My father still has coins _____ he collected a long time ago.

 ⓐ who   ⓑ whom   ⓒ which   ⓓ that

4 What is the name of the fish _____ we ate last night?

 ⓐ who   ⓑ whom   ⓒ which   ⓓ that

B 밑줄 친 관계대명사를 생략할 수 있으면 O, 생략할 수 없으면 X를 쓰세요.

0 This is the computer <u>which</u> my father uses.   O

1 I have a friend <u>who</u> is good at sports.

2 This is the singer <u>whom</u> I like.

3 He is an engineer <u>who</u> designs bridges.

4 Pass me the book <u>which</u> is on the table.

5 The ring <u>which</u> Jane lost was her wedding ring.

6 They are moving a box <u>that</u> looks heavy.

7 John sent the letter <u>which</u> he wrote last night.

8 A parrot is a bird <u>which</u> has colorful feathers.

9 These are flowers <u>that</u> we planted this spring.

WORDS A coin 동전 B bridge 다리, 교량 parrot 앵무새 feather 깃털

C 그림을 보고 who(m) 또는 which와 ( ) 안의 말을 함께 써서 문장을 완성하세요.

0  1 2 3

0 The man _____who(m) I met yesterday_____ spoke Chinese. (I met yesterday)

1 The snowman _____ has melted. (we made)

2 The alarm clock _____ didn't ring this morning.
(I set last night)

3 Nick sent flowers to the girl _____. (he likes)

D 관계대명사를 이용하여 두 문장을 한 문장으로 연결하세요. (who(m) 또는 which를 사용할 것)

0 The shirt is too small for me. I bought it yesterday.
→ The shirt _____which I bought yesterday_____ is too small for me.

1 The dress is beautiful. You are wearing the dress.
→ The dress _____ is beautiful.

2 Susan married a man. She met him at her university.
→ Susan married a man _____.

3 I lost the umbrella. I borrowed it from my friend.
→ I lost the umbrella _____.

4 The students are polite. James teaches the students.
→ The students _____ are polite.

WORDS   C alarm clock 자명종   D marry ~와 결혼하다   university 대학

STEP 1

빈칸 완성 보기에서 알맞은 말을 골라 문장을 완성하세요. (단, 한 번씩만 쓸 것)

보기	who	who	whom	which	which

1 브로콜리는 건강에 좋은 채소이다.

→ Broccoli is a vegetable _____ is good for your health.

2 그 소년이 던진 공이 창문을 깼다.

→ The ball _____ the boy threw broke the window.

3 Sally는 그녀를 도와줄 친구들이 많다.

→ Sally has a lot of friends _____ help her.

4 Jake는 그가 어제 만난 소녀에 대해 이야기했다.

→ Jake talked about the girl _____ he met yesterday.

5 나는 미국으로 이사간 내 친구가 그립다.

→ I miss my friend _____ moved to America.

STEP 2

어구 배열 우리말과 일치하도록 ( ) 안의 말을 알맞게 배열하세요.

6 나는 이 책을 쓴 작가를 만났다. (who, this, wrote, book)

→ I met the writer _____.

7 이것들은 노래하고 춤출 수 있는 로봇이다. (sing, dance, which, and, can)

→ These are robots _____.

8 우리는 Carol이 만든 샌드위치를 먹었다. (made, which, Carol)

→ We ate the sandwiches _____.

9 Jim은 그보다 키가 더 큰 여자친구가 있다. (taller, is, than, who, him)

→ Jim has a girlfriend _____.

10 우리가 어제 본 시험은 어려웠다. (which, took, we, yesterday)

→ The test _____ was difficult.

영작하기 ( ) 안의 말을 이용하여 우리말을 영어로 옮기세요.

11 나는 동물을 사랑하는 사람들이 좋다. (love, animals)

→ I like people _____ .

12 어제 우리가 본 영화는 지루했다. (watch, yesterday)

→ The movie _____ was boring.

13 나는 Tom이 좋아하는 소녀를 안다. (like)

→ I know the girl _____ .

14 이것은 내가 쓴 시이다. (write)

→ This is the poem _____ .

15 보라카이는 아름다운 해변이 많은 섬이다. (have, a lot of, beautiful, beaches)

→ Boracay is an island _____ .

16 그녀는 내가 추천한 책을 읽고 있다. (recommend)

→ She is reading the book _____ .

17 이웃집에 사는 그 여자는 변호사이다. (live, next door)

→ The woman _____ is a lawyer.

18 냉장고에 있던 포도가 어디에 있니? (be, in the refrigerator)

→ Where are the grapes _____ ?

19 내가 인터넷에서 산 신발은 나에게 맞지 않았다. (buy, on the Internet)

→ The shoes _____ didn't fit me.

20 그 뮤지컬은 발레리나가 되고 싶어하는 한 소녀에 관한 것이다. (want, be, a ballerina)

→ The musical is about a girl _____ .

REVIEW TEST
CHAPTER 07

1 빈칸에 들어갈 말이 순서대로 바르게 짝지어진 것은?

> · I have a friend _____ lives in England.
> · He found the book _____ he lost yesterday.

① who – who
② who – that
③ who – whom
④ which – which
⑤ whom – which

서술형

[2-4] 보기에서 알맞은 말을 골라 문장을 완성하시오.
(단, 한 번씩만 쓸 것)

| 보기 | who | whom | which |

2

> The man _____ invited us to dinner was kind.

3

> The opera _____ we watched was boring.

4

> Look at the girl _____ he is talking to.

5 빈칸에 들어갈 말로 알맞은 것은?

> The buses _____ run every hour.

① go to the airport
② that go to the airport
③ who go to the airport
④ that goes to the airport
⑤ which goes to the airport

6 빈칸에 들어갈 말로 알맞지 않은 것은?

> This is the _____ which I like.

① dog
② fruit
③ story
④ teacher
⑤ jacket

7 다음 문장의 밑줄 친 부분과 쓰임이 같은 것은?

> The woman that we met was friendly.

① This is a machine which makes juice.
② The key which is on the table is mine.
③ The woman has a parrot that can talk.
④ The boy who was hungry ate the cake.
⑤ Jim sold the car that he bought last year.

8 밑줄 친 부분을 생략할 수 없는 것은?

① Is this the watch which you lost?
② The fish which he caught was big.
③ He lives in a house that is very old.
④ The man whom you met is my father.
⑤ The coat which Amy is wearing is new.

9 다음 중 관계대명사가 생략된 곳으로 알맞은 것은?

> This is ① the email ② Peter ③ sent ④ me ⑤ yesterday.

10 빈칸에 공통으로 들어갈 말은?

> · People _____ exercise regularly are healthy.
>
> · A koala is an animal _____ lives in Australia.

① they   ② that   ③ who
④ whom   ⑤ which

[11-12] 밑줄 친 부분이 잘못된 것을 고르시오.

11 ① Is this <u>the book you are looking for</u>?
② <u>The boy who scored the goal</u> is Jim.
③ I have <u>a friend which has a twin sister</u>.
④ Look at <u>the girl who is singing a song</u>.
⑤ Dad liked <u>the present which I gave him</u>.

12 ① Tell me <u>the story that you heard</u>.
② He has <u>a son who became a doctor</u>.
③ There was <u>a farmer whom lived alone</u>.
④ I like <u>the shirt which I bought yesterday</u>.
⑤ She is <u>the girl that I met a long time ago</u>.

서술형

13 다음 우리말을 영어로 옮겼을 때 <u>잘못된</u> 부분을 바르게 고쳐서 문장을 다시 쓰시오.

> 나는 엄마가 만든 수프를 좋아한다.
> → I like the soup which my mom makes it.

→ _____

서술형

14 우리말과 일치하도록 ( ) 안의 말을 알맞게 배열하시오.

> 그가 사고 싶은 컴퓨터는 비싸다.
> (the, wants, computer, buy, to, he, which)

→ _____

is expensive.

서술형

[15-16] 우리말과 일치하도록 ( ) 안의 말과 관계대명사를 함께 써서 문장을 완성하시오.

15
> 이것들은 우리 부모님이 재배하는 채소이다.
> (my parents, grow)

→ These are the vegetables

_____.

16
> 경찰은 내 돈을 훔친 남자를 잡았다.
> (steal, my money)

→ The police caught the man

_____.

Appendix 1

불규칙 동사 변화표

A-B-C형

현재	과거	과거분사
be (~이다, 있다)	was/were	been
begin (시작하다)	began	begun
bite (물다)	bit	bitten
blow (불다)	blew	blown
break (깨다)	broke	broken
choose (선택하다)	chose	chosen
do (하다)	did	done
draw (그리다)	drew	drawn
drink (마시다)	drank	drunk
drive (운전하다)	drove	driven
eat (먹다)	ate	eaten
fall (떨어지다)	fell	fallen
fly (날다)	flew	flown
forget (잊다)	forgot	forgotten
get (얻다)	got	got/gotten
give (주다)	gave	given
go (가다)	went	gone
grow (자라다)	grew	grown
hide (숨기다)	hid	hidden
know (알다)	knew	known
ride (타다)	rode	ridden
ring (울리다)	rang	rung
rise (뜨다; 올리다)	rose	risen

현재	과거	과거분사
see (보다)	saw	seen
sing (노래하다)	sang	sung
speak (말하다)	spoke	spoken
steal (훔치다)	stole	stolen
swim (수영하다)	swam	swum
take (잡다)	took	thrown
throw (던지다)	threw	threw
wake (깨우다)	woke	woken
wear (입다)	wore	worn
write (쓰다)	wrote	written

A-B-B형

현재	과거	과거분사
bring (가져오다)	brought	brought
build (짓다)	built	built
buy (사다)	bought	bought
catch (잡다)	caught	caught
feed (먹이다)	fed	fed
feel (느끼다)	felt	felt
fight (싸우다)	fought	fought
find (발견하다)	found	found
hang (걸다)	hung	hung

현재	과거	과거분사
have (가지다)	had	had
hear (듣다)	heard	heard
hold (잡다)	held	held
keep (유지하다)	kept	kept
leave (떠나다)	left	left
lend (빌려주다)	lent	lent
lose (잃다; 지다)	lost	lost
make (만들다)	made	made
meet (만나다)	met	met
pay (지불하다)	paid	paid
say (말하다)	said	said
sell (팔다)	sold	sold
send (보내다)	sent	sent
shine (빛나다)	shone	shone
sit (앉다)	sat	sat
sleep (자다)	slept	slept
spend (소비하다)	spent	spent
stand (서 있다)	stood	stood
teach (가르치다)	taught	taught
tell (말하다)	told	told
think (생각하다)	thought	thought
understand (이해하다)	understood	understood
win (이기다)	won	won

A-B-A형

현재	과거	과거분사
become (되다)	became	become
come (오다)	came	come
run (달리다)	ran	run

A-A-A형

현재	과거	과거분사
cost (비용이 들다)	cost	cost
cut (자르다)	cut	cut
hit (치다)	hit	hit
hurt (다치게 하다)	hurt	hurt
let (시키다)	let	let
put (놓다, 두다)	put	put
quit (그만두다)	quit/quitted	quit/quitted
read (읽다) [ri:d]	read [red]	read [red]
set (놓다)	set	set

Appendix 2

다음 동사의 과거형과 과거분사형을 써서 표를 완성하세요.

A-B-C형

현재	과거	과거분사
be (~이다, 있다)		
begin (시작하다)		
bite (물다)		
blow (불다)		
break (깨다)		
choose (가져오다)		
do (하다)		
draw (그리다)		
drink (마시다)		
drive (운전하다)		
eat (먹다)		
fall (떨어지다)		
fly (날다)		
forget (잊다)		
get (얻다)		
give (주다)		
go (가다)		
grow (자라다)		
hide (숨기다)		
know (알다)		
ride (타다)		
ring (울리다)		
rise (뜨다; 올리다)		

현재	과거	과거분사
see (보다)		
sing (노래하다)		
speak (말하다)		
steal (훔치다)		
swim (수영하다)		
take (잡다)		
throw (던지다)		
wake (깨우다)		
write (쓰다)		

A-B-B형

현재	과거	과거분사
bring (가져오다)		
build (짓다)		
buy (사다)		
catch (잡다)		
feed (먹이다)		
feel (느끼다)		
fight (싸우다)		
find (발견하다)		
hang (걸다)		
have (가지다)		

현재	과거	과거분사
hear (듣다)		
hold (잡다)		
keep (유지하다)		
leave (떠나다)		
lend (빌려주다)		
lose (잃다; 지다)		
make (만들다)		
meet (만나다)		
pay (지불하다)		
say (말하다)		
sell (팔다)		
send (보내다)		
shine (빛나다)		
sit (앉다)		
sleep (자다)		
spend (소비하다)		
stand (서 있다)		
teach (가르치다)		
tell (말하다)		
think (생각하다)		
understand (이해하다)		
wear (입다)		
win (이기다)		

A-B-A형

현재	과거	과거분사
become (되다)		
come (오다)		
run (달리다)		

A-A-A형

현재	과거	과거분사
cost (비용이 들다)		
cut (자르다)		
hit (치다)		
hurt (다치게 하다)		
let (시키다)		
put (놓다, 두다)		
quit (그만두다)		
read (읽다) [ri:d]		
set (놓다)		

MEMO

MEMO

MEMO

Grammar Mate 3

WORKBOOK

Contents

UNIT 01 현재시제, 현재진행형 Present Simple, Present Continuous

A ( ) 안의 말을 이용하여 현재형 문장을 완성하세요.

0   Jisu ____lives____ with a roommate. (live)

1   My brother _____ 178cm tall. (be)

2   We _____ wool from sheep. (get)

3   The baby _____ all the time. (cry)

4   My friend _____ four languages. (speak)

5   I _____ football on Saturdays. (play)

6   Peter _____ a good singer. (not, be)

7   The kids _____ to bed early. (not, go)

8   _____ your parents at home? (be)

9   _____ you _____ vegetables every day? (eat)

B ( ) 안의 말을 이용하여 현재진행형 문장을 완성하세요.

0   I ____am sitting____ on the sofa. (sit)

1   The leaves _____ from the trees. (fall)

2   The cat _____ a nap. (take)

3   The boys _____ the street. (cross)

4   My mother _____ a watermelon. (cut)

5   Some people _____ on the grass. (lie)

6   The teacher _____ on the blackboard. (not, write)

7   The birds _____. (not, fly)

8   _____ he _____ a newspaper? (read)

9   _____ Amy and Paul _____ for a train? (wait)

C ( ) 안에서 알맞은 말을 고르세요.

0   Tyler (works, (is working)) right now.

1   I (know, am knowing) Cindy very well.

2   The dog (eats, is eating) its food now.

3   My mom (hugs, is hugging) me every day.

4   My neighbor (has, is having) two cars.

5   William (wears, is wearing) a tie today.

6   Jane and I (don't study, aren't studying) now.

7   Daniel washes his car (now, once a month).

8   (Do you want, Are you wanting) some cookies?

9   (Does she go, Is she going) to the church every Sunday?

D ( ) 안의 말을 이용하여 우리말을 영어로 옮기세요.

0   어떤 펭귄들은 아프리카에 산다. (live)

　　→ Some penguins _____live_____ in Africa.

1   그 미용사는 내 머리를 자르고 있다. (cut)

　　→ The hairdresser _____ my hair.

2   그녀는 이메일을 쓰고 있니? (write)

　　→ _____ an email?

3   그는 밤에는 커피를 마시지 않는다. (drink)

　　→ He _____ coffee at night.

4   너는 잠옷을 입고 자니? (wear)

　　→ _____ pajamas to bed?

UNIT 02 과거시제, 과거진행형 Past Simple, Past Continuous

A ( ) 안에서 알맞은 말을 고르세요.

0   I (am, (was)) unhappy last week.

1   You (are, were) 14 years old now.

2   Judy (is, was) in Florida last summer.

3   They (are, were) at the zoo yesterday.

4   Alex (eats, ate) chicken last night.

5   My brother and I (go, went) skiing every winter.

6   They (work, worked) hard last year.

7   Amy (helps, helped) her mother this morning.

8   I (don't speak, didn't speak) English well last year.

9   (Do they enjoy, Did they enjoy) the party yesterday?

B ( ) 안의 말을 이용하여 현재진행형 또는 과거진행형 문장을 완성하세요.

0   I _____ was cleaning _____ my room then. (clean)

1   Kate and I _____ TV now. (watch)

2   You _____ an hour ago. (sleep)

3   It _____ all day yesterday. (rain)

4   Emily _____ a picture now. (draw)

5   Let's go home. It _____ dark. (get)

6   They _____ right now. (not, study)

7   They _____ at that time. (not, study)

8   _____ he _____ to school now? (go)

9   What _____ you _____ at this time yesterday? (do)

C 빈칸에 did/didn't, was/wasn't, were/weren't 중 알맞은 것을 넣어 대화를 완성하세요.

0   A: _____Were_____ you reading a book?

B: No, I _____wasn't_____.

1   A: _____ he write a letter to Jane?

B: Yes, he _____.

2   A: _____ they speaking Chinese?

B: No, they _____.

3   A: _____ Kate buy that dress?

B: No, she _____.

4   A: _____ the children singing a song?

B: Yes, they _____.

D ( ) 안의 말을 이용하여 우리말을 영어로 옮기세요.

0   나는 오래 전에 이 곳에 살았다. (live)

→ I _____lived_____ here long time ago.

1   그 차는 너무 빨리 달리고 있었다. (run)

→ The car _____ too fast.

2   그 복사기는 잘 작동하지 않았다. (work)

→ The copy machine _____ well.

3   너는 주말을 잘 보냈니? (have)

→ _____ a nice weekend?

4   그들은 공원에서 배드민턴을 치고 있었니? (play)

→ _____ badminton in the park?

03 현재완료 1 Present Perfect 1

A 주어진 동사의 과거형과 과거분사형을 쓰세요.

0	have	–	had	–	had
1	visit	–		–	
2	do	–		–	
3	eat	–		–	
4	write	–		–	
5	meet	–		–	
6	buy	–		–	
7	come	–		–	
8	run	–		–	
9	cut	–		–	

B ( ) 안의 말을 이용하여 현재완료 문장을 완성하세요.

0 The snowman _____has melted_____. (melt)

1 All the guests _____. (arrive)

2 My father _____ his car. (not, sell)

3 Lucy and Mike _____ swimming. (go)

4 Anna _____ her bag. (lose)

5 I _____ many books this year. (not, read)

6 Eric _____ as a tour guide for two years. (work)

7 His son _____ sick since Monday. (be)

8 Somebody _____ the window. (break)

9 They _____ that puzzle. (not, finish)

C 보기에서 알맞은 말을 골라 현재완료 의문문과 대답을 완성하세요. (단, 한 번씩만 쓸 것)

보기	~~check~~	hear	leave	see	study

0 A: _____Has_____ Mr. Kim _____checked_____ his email?

B: No, he _____hasn't_____. Maybe he forgot.

1 A: _____ you _____ that movie?

B: No, I _____. Is it interesting?

2 A: _____ the train _____ the station?

B: Yes, it _____. Let's wait for the next train.

3 A: _____ they _____ for the test?

B: Yes, they _____. I saw them in the library.

4 A: _____ you _____ the news about Sam?

B: No, I _____. What is it?

D ( ) 안의 말을 이용하여 우리말을 영어로 옮기세요. (현재완료를 사용할 것)

0 그들은 하루 종일 아무것도 먹지 않았다. (eat)

→ They _____haven't eaten_____ anything all day.

1 비가 그쳤니? (stop)

→ _____ the rain _____?

2 그는 아직 내 질문에 대답하지 않았다. (answer)

→ He _____ my question yet.

3 Andrew는 지금까지 많은 나라를 여행했다. (travel)

→ Andrew _____ to many countries so far.

4 너는 잃어버린 열쇠를 찾았니? (find)

→ _____ you _____ the missing key?

현재완료 2 Present Perfect 2

A ( ) 안의 말을 이용하여 현재완료 문장을 완성하세요.

0 The mail _____ has _____ just _____ arrived _____. (arrive)

1 Eva _____ her lunch yet. (not, finish)

2 Danny and Susan _____ already _____ the house. (clean)

3 _____ you ever _____ a panda before? (see)

4 Kelly _____ never _____ French food. (eat)

5 I _____ a mountain twice. (climb)

6 Bob _____ the same job for ten years. (have)

7 Kelly _____ in the hospital since last Monday. (be)

8 Henry's family _____ to Canada. (go)

9 Julie _____ the library book. (lose)

B ( ) 안에서 알맞은 말을 고르세요.

0 Have you ever (go, gone) water-skiing?

1 Tim (has been, was) very busy last week.

2 Daniel (has been, went) to Australia once.

3 The leaves (haven't, didn't) turned brown yet.

4 Mike (has ridden, rode) his bike to school yesterday.

5 A: (Have, Did) you met Harry before? B: Yes, I (have, did).

6 Helen and Jack (have left, left) home an hour ago.

7 How long (have you had, did you have) long hair?

8 My mom is a good driver. She (has driven, drove) her car for many years.

9 A: Have you (done, did) your homework? B: Yes, I (have, did).

C 보기에서 알맞은 말을 골라 문장을 완성하세요. (단, 한 번씩만 쓸 것)

> 보기   ago   yet   ~~ever~~

0   Have you _____ever_____ tried bungee jumping?

1   They moved to a new house two weeks _____.

2   My sister and I haven't washed the dishes _____.

> 보기   for   since   last night

3   Kate is my best friend. I have known her _____ 10 years.

4   Mike went to bed at 11:30 _____.

5   He has written several books _____ 2010.

D ( ) 안의 말을 이용하여 우리말을 영어로 옮기세요.

0   나는 미국에 가 본 적이 있다. (be)

→ I _____have been_____ to America.

1   너는 무지개를 본 적이 있니? (ever, see)

→ _____ a rainbow?

2   아직 봄이 오지 않았다. (come)

→ Spring _____ yet.

3   비행기가 방금 공항에 착륙했다. (just, land)

→ The plane _____ at the airport.

4   나는 기타를 쳐 본 적이 한 번도 없다. (never, play)

→ I _____ the guitar.

To부정사 To-Infinitives

A 밑줄 친 to부정사의 역할로 알맞은 것을 보기에서 고르세요.

보기　　ⓐ 주어　　ⓑ 목적어　　ⓒ 보어

0	My dream is <u>to be</u> a pianist.	→ ⓒ
1	Do you want <u>to visit</u> the museum?	→
2	<u>To learn</u> English is not easy.	→
3	It is dangerous <u>to cross</u> the road at a red light.	→
4	We need <u>to buy</u> some food.	→
5	It is difficult <u>to answer</u> the question.	→
6	Karen's job is <u>to write</u> stories for children.	→
7	<u>To exercise</u> regularly is good for your health.	→
8	His goal is <u>to lose</u> 10 kilograms.	→
9	They decided <u>to move</u> to a new house.	→

B 밑줄 친 to부정사가 꾸미는 말에 동그라미 하세요.

0 I have (a present) <u>to give</u> you.

1 There are lots of things <u>to see</u> in New York.

2 The boy has no friends <u>to play</u> with.

3 What is the best way <u>to get</u> to the station?

4 Karen always takes a book <u>to read</u>.

5 Do you want something <u>to drink</u>?

6 It is time <u>to go</u> home.

7 She has three puppies <u>to take</u> care of.

Ⓒ 자연스러운 문장이 되도록 알맞게 연결하세요.

0	We ran •	• ⓐ to go out.
1	I called my friend •	• ⓑ to buy a new car.
2	She went to the park •	• ⓒ to pass the exam.
3	He is saving money •	• ⓓ to walk her dog.
4	I was sorry •	• ⓔ to catch the last bus.
5	They were happy •	• ⓕ to check the weather.
6	He turned off the light •	• ⓖ to ask about our homework.
7	She opened the window •	• ⓗ to hear the sad news.

Ⓓ ( ) 안의 말을 이용하여 우리말을 영어로 옮기세요. (to부정사를 사용할 것)

0 우리에게 먹을 것이 아무것도 없다. (nothing, eat)

→ We have _____nothing to eat_____.

1 우리는 수영을 하기 위해 바다에 갔다. (swim)

→ We went to the sea _____.

2 영화를 보는 것은 재미있다. (watch)

→ _____ is fun _____ a movie.

3 내 목표는 중국어를 배우는 것이다. (learn)

→ My goal is _____ Chinese.

4 나는 그 결과를 받고 기뻤다. (happy, get)

→ I was _____ the results.

06 동명사 Gerunds

A 밑줄 친 동명사의 역할로 알맞은 것을 보기에서 고르세요.

보기   ⓐ 주어   ⓑ 목적어   ⓒ 보어

0   Sally finished <u>reading</u> the book.   →   ⓑ

1   <u>Being</u> kind to others is important.   →

2   My hobby is <u>playing</u> the guitar.   →

3   The passengers had to keep <u>waiting</u>.   →

4   Do you mind <u>turning</u> on the air conditioner?   →

5   Her favorite activity is <u>singing</u>.   →

6   We gave up <u>finding</u> the house.   →

7   <u>Doing</u> yoga is a great way to relax.   →

8   <u>Eating</u> sweets is bad for your teeth.   →

B ( ) 안에서 알맞은 말을 모두 고르세요.

0   I hope (going, (to go)) to Hawaii again.

1   Sam is learning (driving, to drive) a car.

2   We need (doing, to do) something to help them.

3   Do you enjoy (going, to go) to the beach in summer?

4   What do you want (being, to be) in the future?

5   Mina practiced (dancing, to dance) all day.

6   Most people hate (working, to work) on holidays.

7   The band started (playing, to play) music.

8   Do you promise (studying, to study) harder?

9   Eric is good at (cooking, to cook) Chinese food.

C 보기에서 알맞은 말을 골라 적절한 형태로 바꾸어 대화를 완성하세요. (단, 한 번씩만 쓸 것)

| 보기 | do | go | read | ski | travel |

0   A: What do you do in your free time?

    B: I enjoy _____reading_____ novels.

1   A: What is your favorite sport?

    B: My favorite sport is _____.

2   A: Do you mind _____ by plane?

    B: No, I prefer traveling by train.

3   A: What are you planning _____ on Christmas Day?

    B: I'm going to see a musical.

4   A: Why didn't you eat the cake?

    B: I've decided _____ on a diet.

D ( ) 안의 말을 이용하여 우리말을 영어로 옮기세요. (동명사를 사용할 것)

0   나는 사진 찍는 것을 좋아한다. (take)

    → I like _____taking_____ pictures.

1   영어로 편지를 쓰는 것은 쉽지 않다. (write)

    → _____ a letter in English is not easy.

2   음악을 듣는 것은 휴식을 취하는 좋은 방법이다. (listen)

    → _____ to music is a good way to relax.

3   그 아이들은 바다에서 수영하는 것을 즐긴다. (swim)

    → The kids enjoy _____ in the sea.

4   그녀는 매일 피아노 치는 것을 연습한다. (play)

    → She practices _____ the piano every day.

여러 가지 동사 1 Various Verbs 1

A ( ) 안에서 알맞은 말을 고르세요.

0   She (looks, sounds) pretty today.

1   This soup (smells, sounds) good.

2   The math class (sounds, tastes) boring.

3   This fruit (feels, tastes) sweet.

4   The wooden table (feels, sounds) smooth.

5   The cat looks (sleep, sleepy).

6   Her voice sounds (love, lovely).

7   The fish smells (terrible, terribly).

8   Ann (felt, felt like) sick this morning.

9   I (feel, feel like) a movie star.

B ( ) 안의 말을 알맞게 배열하여 문장을 완성하세요.

0   The news _____made the family sad_____. (sad, the family, made)

1   The mosquito _____ all night. (me, awake, kept)

2   Can I _____? (Tom, you, call)

3   The chef _____. (the food, warm, kept)

4   The TV show _____. (famous, made, her)

5   I _____. (my computer, broken, found)

6   They _____. (him, elected, their next leader)

7   John _____. (his dog, Teddy, named)

8   You should _____. (the classroom, clean, keep)

9   Susan _____. (found, easy, her homework)

C 밑줄 친 부분이 맞으면 O를 쓰고, 틀리면 바르게 고치세요.

0	Your jacket looks <u>nicely</u>.	→	nice
1	The beef stew smells <u>greatly</u>.	→	
2	The floor felt <u>coldly</u>.	→	
3	Her voice sounds <u>lovely</u>.	→	
4	The cello <u>sounds</u> wonderful.	→	
5	The baby <u>looks</u> an angel.	→	
6	I found the book <u>interestingly</u>.	→	
7	He made the soup <u>salty</u>.	→	
8	Happiness keeps you <u>health</u>.	→	
9	His friends call <u>he</u> Dave.	→	

D ( ) 안의 말을 이용하여 우리말을 영어로 옮기세요.

0   그 강아지들은 귀여워 보인다. (cute)

→ The puppies _____ look cute _____.

1   그녀의 목소리는 친근하게 들린다. (friendly)

→ Her voice _____.

2   지구 온난화는 지구를 더 덥게 만든다. (the Earth, hotter)

→ Global warming _____.

3   아이들을 조용히 시켜주세요. (the children, quiet)

→ Please _____.

4   그는 항상 나를 Peter라고 부른다. (Peter)

→ He always _____.

여러 가지 동사 2 Various Verbs 2

A 주어진 문장의 형태로 알맞은 것을 보기에서 고르세요.

보기	ⓐ 주어 + 동사 + 간접목적어 + 직접목적어
	ⓑ 주어 + 동사 + 직접목적어 + 전치사 + 간접목적어

0 Mr. Kim always gives us homework. → ⓐ

1 He sent me a postcard from Peru. →

2 Can you pass me the water bottle? →

3 He wrote a letter to me. →

4 My dad bought me a new scooter. →

5 Susan made dinner for us. →

6 Will you lend me 10 dollars? →

7 I won't show my report card to my parents. →

8 The police officer asked some questions of him. →

9 He told us the story of his trip. →

B ( ) 안의 말을 알맞게 배열하여 문장을 완성하세요.

0 I will _____write Sam a letter_____. (a letter, Sam, write)

1 Ellie _____. (us, bought, pizza)

2 Bill _____. (a paper airplane, his brother, made)

3 She _____. (her address, me, gave)

4 He _____. (passed, the ball, me)

5 Mr. Timber _____. (teaches, math, us)

6 My friend _____. (me, an invitation, sent)

7 The waiter _____. (some ice, brought, us)

C 두 문장의 뜻이 같도록 빈칸에 알맞은 말을 써서 문장을 완성하세요.

0 The man showed us the city map.

→ The man showed the city map _____to us_____.

1 My grandma bought me a nice coat.

→ My grandma bought a nice coat _____.

2 Tracy lent me her sneakers.

→ Tracy lent her sneakers _____.

3 I made Susie an apple pie.

→ I made an apple pie _____.

4 I won't ask you any more questions.

→ I won't ask any more questions _____.

D ( ) 안의 말을 이용하여 우리말을 영어로 옮기세요.

0 Chen은 나에게 중국어를 가르쳐주었다. (teach, Chinese)

→ Chen _____taught me Chinese_____.

1 나의 선생님은 나에게 책 한 권을 주셨다. (give, a book)

→ My teacher _____.

2 그녀는 나에게 코코아 한 잔을 타주었다. (make, a cup of cocoa)

→ She _____.

3 우리 엄마는 나에게 새 휴대폰을 사주지 않을 것이다. (buy, a new cellphone)

→ My mom won't _____.

4 리모컨 좀 가져다 줄래? (bring, the remote control)

→ Can you _____?

수동태 1 The Passive 1

A 밑줄 친 부분의 의미로 알맞은 것을 고르세요.

0 The email <u>was written</u> by Jack. ☐ 썼다 ☑ 쓰여졌다

1 Somebody <u>broke</u> the window. ☐ 깼다 ☐ 깨졌다

2 Pine trees <u>were planted</u> in the park. ☐ 심었다 ☐ 심어졌다

3 Many children <u>use</u> their cellphones. ☐ 사용한다 ☐ 사용된다

4 Ketchup <u>is made</u> from tomatoes. ☐ 만든다 ☐ 만들어진다

5 He <u>delivers</u> milk every morning. ☐ 배달한다 ☐ 배달된다

6 The picnic <u>was canceled</u> yesterday. ☐ 취소했다 ☐ 취소되었다

7 The Wright brothers <u>invented</u> the first plane. ☐ 발명했다 ☐ 발명되었다

8 The bridge <u>was built</u> in 1987. ☐ 지었다 ☐ 지어졌다

9 This song <u>is sung</u> by many people. ☐ 부른다 ☐ 불린다

B ( ) 안에서 알맞은 말을 고르세요.

0 The bird (ate, was eaten) the worm.

1 The report (finished, was finished) by Susan.

2 The thief (caught, was caught) by the police.

3 Mr. Black (saw, was seen) the accident.

4 Somebody (took, was taken) my book.

5 Ron and I (invite, were invited) to Carl's party.

6 The class (teaches, is taught) by Mr. Brown.

7 The building (destroyed, was destroyed) by the fire.

8 The money (stole, was stolen) by someone.

9 The man (found, was found) my wallet for me.

C 우리말과 일치하도록 ( ) 안의 말을 알맞게 배열하세요.

0 그 케이크는 내가 구웠다. (was, the cake, baked, me, by)

→ _____ The cake was baked by me. _____

1 이 책은 많은 사람들에게 읽힌다. (many people, read, this book, is, by)

→ _____

2 그 편지들은 이틀 전에 보내졌다. (the letters, sent, were, two days ago)

→ _____

3 그 어린 소년은 개에게 물렸다. (was, by, the little boy, bitten, a dog)

→ _____

4 그 셔츠는 Tim이 다렸다. (Tim, ironed, the shirt, by, was)

→ _____

D ( ) 안의 말을 이용하여 우리말을 영어로 옮기세요.

0 많은 영화들이 할리우드에서 만들어진다. (make)

→ Many movies _____ are made _____ in Hollywood.

1 그의 차는 한 달에 한 번 세차된다. (wash)

→ His car _____ once a month.

2 그 세탁기는 어제 고쳐졌다. (fix)

→ The washing machine _____ yesterday.

3 나의 새 휴대폰은 지난 주에 도난 당했다. (steal)

→ My new cellphone _____ last week.

4 그 크리스마스 카드들은 매년 12월 1일에 보내진다. (send)

→ The Christmas cards _____ on December 1 every year.

10 수동태 2 The Passive 2

A 보기에서 알맞은 말을 골라 적절한 형태로 바꾸어 수동태 문장을 완성하세요. (현재형 또는 과거형으로 쓸 것)

보기	clean	find	hit	invite	paint	play	produce	use

0 The key _____was found_____ in my bag.

1 Milk _____ by cows.

2 The child _____ by a car last night.

3 That picture _____ by Picasso.

4 Football _____ all over the world.

5 Chopsticks _____ in many Asian countries.

6 My shoes _____ by me every day.

7 About 200 people _____ to the wedding.

B 주어진 문장을 밑줄 친 부분을 주어로 하는 수동태 문장으로 바꿔 쓰세요.

0 Ian broke the crystal vase.

→ _____The crystal vase was broken by Ian._____

1 Someone stole his money.

→ _____

2 The mechanic repairs cars.

→ _____

3 She closed the door.

→ _____

4 The actress wore the dress.

→ _____

C 주어진 문장을 밑줄 친 부분을 주어로 하는 능동태 문장으로 바꿔 쓰세요.

0 The note was written by <u>my mom</u>.

→ _____ My mom wrote the note. _____

1 The president is elected by <u>the people</u>.

→ _____

2 The TV was turned on by <u>us</u>.

→ _____

3 The swimming pool is used by <u>the hotel guests</u>.

→ _____

4 The blackboard was erased by <u>the teacher</u>.

→ _____

D ( ) 안의 말을 이용하여 우리말을 영어로 옮기세요.

0 그 만화 영화는 많은 사람들에게 사랑을 받았다. (love)

→ The animation _____ was loved _____ by many people.

1 그 돈은 안전한 장소에 보관된다. (keep)

→ The money _____ in a safe place.

2 그 케이크는 Sally에 의해 잘렸다. (cut)

→ The cake _____ by Sally.

3 그 남자는 뱀에게 물렸다. (bite)

→ The man _____ by a snake.

4 Mike는 그 파티에 초대되지 않았다. (not, invite)

→ Mike _____ to the party.

A ( ) 안에서 알맞은 말을 고르세요.

0   My brother (and, but) I are good at sports.

1   The flag is red, blue, white, (and, or) black.

2   Do you want a Coke (but, or) lemonade?

3   The old man walked slowly (and, or) carefully.

4   Do you go to school by bus (but, or) on foot?

5   You can cut the string with scissors (or, so) a knife.

6   It was very warm, (but, so) we went swimming.

7   The girl fell over, (but, or) she didn't cry.

8   Lucia is from Canada, (but, so) she lives in Korea.

9   Mom is sick today, (or, so) Dad will pick me up after school.

B 보기에서 알맞은 말을 골라 문장을 완성하세요. (중복 가능)

보기	and	but	or	so

0   Nancy likes sweets _____and_____ chocolates.

1   Is your sister older _____ younger than you?

2   He bought some apples, oranges, _____ pears.

3   I called Kevin, _____ he didn't answer.

4   It started raining, _____ we went to a café.

5   Next year, Alice will work in Canada _____ in Australia.

6   Vicky likes music, _____ she doesn't like sports.

7   I'm very hungry, _____ I can eat all the sandwiches.

C ( ) 안의 말을 이용하여 두 문장을 한 문장으로 만드세요.

0 Mike loves Cathy. She loves someone else. (but)

→ _____Mike loves Cathy, but she loves someone else._____

1 She can play the piano. She can play the guitar. (and)

→ _____

2 The line was long. We waited for a long time. (so)

→ _____

3 Do you want to go with us? Do you want to stay here? (or)

→ _____

4 He got a cold. He didn't take any medicine. (but)

→ _____

D ( ) 안의 말을 이용하여 우리말을 영어로 옮기세요.

0 그 바닥은 물기가 있고 미끄러웠다. (wet, slippery)

→ The floor was _____wet and slippery_____.

1 시간이 늦어서, 나는 엄마에게 전화를 했다. (call)

→ It was late, _____ my mom.

2 그 시계는 비쌌지만, 나는 그것을 샀다. (buy)

→ The watch was expensive, _____ it.

3 우리는 눈싸움을 하고 눈사람을 만들었다. (make, a snowman)

→ We had a snowball fight _____.

4 너는 지금 숙제를 할거니 아니면 나중에 할거니? (now, later)

→ Will you do your homework _____?

A ( ) 안에서 알맞은 말을 고르세요.

0 (If, After) it rains, we won't go hiking.

1 The sun was shining (when, if) he woke up.

2 I met an old friend (after, while) I was walking home.

3 He fastened his seatbelt (after, if) he got in the car.

4 I put on my pajamas (before, while) I go to bed.

5 Close all the windows (before, because) you go out.

6 My dog wags its tail (when, before) I get home.

7 I can't read anything (after, if) I don't wear glasses.

8 We saw lions and tigers (when, if) we went to the zoo.

9 Ted did all the housework (because, before) his wife was sick.

B 보기에서 알맞은 말을 골라 문장을 완성하세요. (단, 한 번씩만 쓸 것)

보기	~~when~~	after	because

0 He was five _____when_____ his father died.

1 She closed the book _____ it was boring.

2 You can have dessert _____ you finish your meal.

보기	while	before	if

3 She woke up _____ her baby was crying.

4 _____ I see Helen, I will give her your message.

5 We bought some popcorn _____ we watched the movie.

C ( ) 안의 말을 이용하여 두 문장을 한 문장으로 만드세요.

0 You must stop your car. The light turns red. (when)

→ _____ You must stop your car when the light turns red. _____

1 I was playing soccer. I hurt my ankle. (while)

→ _____

2 She felt sick. She ate the fish. (after)

→ _____

3 He called the police. He lost his wallet. (because)

→ _____

4 I will walk to school. The weather is good. (if)

→ _____

D ( ) 안의 말을 이용하여 우리말을 영어로 옮기세요.

0 그녀는 뛰다가 넘어졌다. (run)

→ She fell down _____ while she was running _____.

1 그는 방을 나가기 전에 컴퓨터를 껐다. (leave)

→ He turned off the computer _____ the room.

2 내가 어렸을 때, 나는 자주 나의 형과 싸웠다. (young)

→ _____, I often fought with my brother.

3 나는 숙제를 끝마친 후에 TV를 볼 것이다. (finish)

→ I will watch TV _____ my homework.

4 Angela가 나를 초대한다면, 나는 파티에 갈 것이다. (invite)

→ _____, I will go to the party.

A 형용사절에는 밑줄을 치고, 형용사절이 꾸미는 말에는 동그라미 하세요.

0   (The boy) who is crossing the street is Jim.

1   Cindy buys milk that is low fat.

2   I have an aunt who lives in Seattle.

3   Grace is the girl who is wearing the red dress.

4   The man who is in the kitchen is my father.

5   Tony is wearing jeans that are too tight.

6   The cat which scratched me is Sally's.

7   The person who sent the roses is Chris.

8   Amy bought a bag which cost $20.

9   Is there a shop which sells swimsuits?

B ( ) 안에서 알맞은 말을 고르세요.

0   I don't like food (who, (that)) is too sweet.

1   The man (who, which) answered the phone was polite.

2   My neighbor has a dog (who, which) barks a lot.

3   Is there a car (who, that) runs on water?

4   A coffeemaker is a machine (who, which) makes coffee.

5   The man (who, which) sang at the concert has a good voice.

6   She is the woman (who, which) works in the library.

7   He works for a company (who, which) makes computers.

8   The people (who, which) sat next to me were noisy.

9   Did you see the man (who, which) stole your bag?

C 관계대명사를 이용하여 두 문장을 한 문장으로 만드세요. (who 또는 which를 사용할 것)

0 The man was brave. He saved the kid.

→ _____ The man who saved the kid was brave. _____

1 I bought a dress. It was on sale.

→ _____

2 Do you see the cat? It is on the roof.

→ _____

3 The girl was Karen. She came here.

→ _____

4 She took out the ring. It was in the box.

→ _____

D ( ) 안의 말을 이용하여 우리말을 영어로 옮기세요. (who 또는 which를 사용할 것)

0 어젯밤에 내린 눈이 녹고 있다. (fall, last night)

→ The snow _____ which fell last night _____ is melting.

1 우리에게 서빙을 한 웨이터는 친절했다. (serve, us)

→ The waiter _____ was kind.

2 이것은 물을 따뜻하게 유지시켜주는 병이다. (keep, water, warm)

→ This is a bottle _____.

3 영어를 할 수 있는 사람이 있나요? (can, speak, English)

→ Is there anyone _____?

4 그 사고를 목격한 남자는 경찰을 불렀다. (see, accident)

→ The man _____ called the police.

UNIT 14 관계대명사 2 Relative Pronouns 2

A 밑줄 친 관계대명사가 주격인지 목적격인지 고르세요.

		주격	목적격
0	The eggs <u>which</u> she bought are bad.	☐	☑
1	The man <u>whom</u> I met was a doctor.	☐	☐
2	The woman <u>who</u> said hello is our new teacher.	☐	☐
3	He has everything <u>that</u> he wants.	☐	☐
4	I go to school <u>which</u> is near my house.	☐	☐
5	The musician <u>who</u> wrote this song is young.	☐	☐
6	The car <u>that</u> John uses is his uncle's.	☐	☐
7	Fish are animals <u>that</u> live in water.	☐	☐
8	My grandfather likes the cookies <u>which</u> I make.	☐	☐
9	Ann visited her friend <u>who</u> lives in a different city.	☐	☐

B ( ) 안에서 알맞은 말을 고르세요.

0 Everything (whom, (which)) he said was a lie.

1 The laptop (who, which) he bought is broken.

2 Susan is someone (which, that) I can trust.

3 The boy (whom, which) we met is from Japan.

4 Here is the drink (who, that) you ordered.

5 Is this the book (whom, that) you lost?

6 Tom wrote a letter to a girl (whom, which) he likes.

7 I liked the meal (who, which) we ate for lunch.

8 The question (whom, which) he asked me was interesting.

9 I corrected the mistakes (whom, that) I made in the letter.

C 관계대명사를 이용하여 두 문장을 한 문장으로 만드세요. (who(m) 또는 which를 사용할 것)

0 The girl was pretty. I met her yesterday.

→ _____ The girl who(m) I met yesterday was pretty. _____

1 The cup was broken. He dropped it.

→ _____

2 She gave me the strawberry jam. She made it.

→ _____

3 The teacher is Mrs. Yoon. I like her the most.

→ _____

4 This is the tree. My dad and I planted it.

→ _____

D ( ) 안의 말을 이용하여 우리말을 영어로 옮기세요. (who(m) 또는 which를 사용할 것)

0 이것은 내가 사고 싶은 컴퓨터이다. (want, buy)

→ This is the computer _____ which I want to buy _____.

1 나는 우리 엄마가 나에게 준 목걸이를 잃어버렸다. (my mom, give)

→ I lost the necklace _____.

2 그는 나에게 그가 찍은 사진들을 보여주었다. (take)

→ He showed me the photos _____.

3 그가 좋아하는 소녀는 그의 반 친구이다. (like)

→ The girl _____ is his classmate.

4 Mary는 내가 매일 만나는 친구이다. (meet)

→ Mary is a friend _____ every day.

Grammar Mate 3

Grammar Mate is a three-level grammar series for intermediate learners. This series is designed to help students understand basic English grammar with various step-by-step exercises. All chapters offer writing exercises to strengthen students' writing abilities and grammatical accuracy as well as review tests to prepare them for actual school tests. This series can be used by teachers in the classroom, by tutors teaching a small group of students, and by students for self-study purposes. With this series, students will improve their confidence in English. In addition, they will develop a solid foundation in English grammar to prepare themselves for a more advanced level.

Key Features

- Core basic English grammar
- Easy, clear explanations of grammar rules and concepts
- Plenty of various step-by-step exercises
- Writing exercises to develop writing skills and grammatical accuracy
- Comprehensive tests to prepare for actual school tests
- Workbook for further practice

Components Student Book | Workbook | Answer Key

Online Resources : www.darakwon.co.kr

Vocabulary Lists & Tests | Sentence Lists & Tests | Extra Exercises | Midterm & Final Exams

Grammar Mate Series

 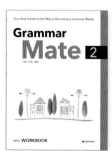 

Grammar Mate 3

〰〰〰

ANSWER KEY

CHAPTER
01

Present & Past Tenses
현재시제와 과거시제

UNIT 01 현재시제, 현재진행형
Present Simple,
Present Continuous

LET'S CHECK
p.13, 15

A

1 learn 2 live 3 takes 4 buys 5 sells
6 is 7 are 8 comes 9 study

B

1 I don't know the answer to the question.
2 Are the students at the library?
3 Do they have a lot of free time?
4 My mother doesn't drive a car.

C

1 is painting 2 is making 3 is running
4 are lying 5 are flying

D

1 aren't speaking 2 isn't moving
3 isn't doing 4 Am, singing 5 Are, wearing
6 Is, coming 7 Are, playing

LET'S PRACTICE
p.16-17

A

1 build 2 don't 3 listen 4 cries 5 Do
6 is 7 are 8 Does 9 visits

B

1 She is going shopping.
2 Is he running fast?
3 I'm not[I am not] washing the dishes.
4 Mike isn't[is not] buying clothes.

C

1 draw 2 is smiling 3 order 4 is driving
5 has 6 need 7 is sitting 8 take
9 am studying

D

1 Do 2 are 3 doesn't 4 teach 5 want
6 is rising 7 are waiting 8 Do you know
9 isn't raining

UNIT 02 과거시제, 과거진행형
Past Simple, Past Continuous

LET'S CHECK
p.19, 21

A

1 bought 2 collect 3 is 4 sank
5 wrote 6 delivers 7 is 8 passed
9 missed

B

1 Were they busy on Monday?
2 We didn't go to the baseball game yesterday.
3 Did you enjoy the movie?
4 Did he get a haircut yesterday?

C

1 was helping 2 was ringing
3 were jumping 4 were running
5 was playing 6 was drinking
7 were having 8 were cleaning
9 was making

D

1 wasn't waiting 2 weren't watching
3 weren't fighting 4 wasn't wearing
5 Was, taking 6 Was, buying
7 Were, swimming 8 Were, eating
9 Was, riding

LET'S PRACTICE
p.22-23

A

1 arrived 2 was, sells 3 got 4 traveled
5 was 6 are 7 was 8 is 9 was

B

1 was eating lunch
2 was playing soccer
3 was reading a book

C

1 Was / wasn't, was 2 Were / were, were
3 Did / didn't, was 4 Did / didn't, didn't

D

1 was sleeping　2 wasn't　3 didn't
4 meet　5 walking　6 wasn't　7 moved
8 run　9 Did

LET'S WRITE

STEP 1

1 wear　2 invented　3 standing　4 were
5 knows

STEP 2

6 My grandparents live in the country.
7 I finished my homework an hour ago.
8 He was surfing the Internet.
9 Jessica is watering the flowers.
10 I didn't speak English well.

STEP 3

11 My grandmother is 70 years old this year.
12 He was my P.E. teacher last year.
13 They eat out on Fridays.
14 My family went on a picnic last weekend.
15 I don't believe in ghosts.
16 Did you buy a new computer yesterday?
17 Tom is waiting for his friends.
18 The children were playing a board game.
19 Is she practicing the piano?
20 Were they sitting on the sofa?

REVIEW TEST

1 ②　2 ①　3 ④
4 doesn't[does not] have
5 Was she studying　6 ②　7 ①　8 ④
9 ③　10 ③　11 ⑤　12 ③
13 visited　14 Are you making
15 doesn't[does not] stop
16 were jumping　17 Did he catch

해설

1 변함없는 진리는 현재시제로 나타낸다. 주어(Water)가 3인칭 단수이므로 동사원형에 -(e)s를 붙인다.

2 10 minutes ago는 과거를 나타내므로 leave의 과거형인 ① left가 알맞다.

3 at the moment(지금은)는 현재진행형과 어울리는 시간 표현이다. 현재진행형은 「be동사의 현재형 + 동사원형-ing」 형태이므로 ④ is watching이 알맞다.

4 일반동사 현재형의 부정문은 「don't/doesn't + 동사원형」 형태이다. 주어가 The man이므로 doesn't[does not] have가 알맞다.

5 과거진행형 의문문은 「be동사의 과거형 + 주어 + 동사원형-ing?」 형태이다. 따라서 Was she studying이 알맞다.

6 현재진행형은 「be동사의 현재형 + 동사원형-ing」 형태이다. 주어가 She이므로 cuts를 is cutting으로 고쳐야 알맞다.

7 일반동사 과거형의 의문문은 「Did + 주어 + 동사원형?」 형태이다. 따라서 ① Did he go to school by bus?가 알맞다.

8 ①②③⑤는 모두 과거를 나타내는 시간 표현이 쓰였으므로 was, ④는 지금(now) 진행 중인 일이므로 is가 알맞다.

9 빈칸 뒤에 형용사 tall이 있으므로 빈칸에는 be동사가 와야 한다. 내용상 과거와 현재의 일을 나타내므로 ③ wasn't – am이 알맞다.

10 어제의 일을 묻는 내용이다. 일반동사 find가 쓰였으므로 조동사 did를 사용해서 묻고 답한다.

11 상태 동사는 현재진행형을 쓰지 않고 현재시제를 쓴다. 따라서 ① is having → has, ② I'm wanting → I want, ③ Are you knowing → Do you know, ④ is liking → likes로 고쳐야 알맞다. ⑤의 have는 '먹다'의 의미이므로 진행형을 쓸 수 있다.

12 ① not fly → don't fly, ② isn't sell → doesn't sell, ④ didn't cleaned → didn't clean, ⑤ don't eating → aren't eating으로 고쳐야 알맞다.

13 last weekend는 과거를 나타내므로 visit → visited로 고쳐야 알맞다.

14 지금(now) 진행 중인 일을 묻고 있다. 현재진행형 의문문은 「be동사의 현재형 + 주어 + 동사원형-ing?」 형태이므로 Do you make → Are you making으로 고쳐야 알맞다.

15 일반동사 현재형의 부정문은 「don't/doesn't + 동사원형」 형태이다. 주어가 The elevator이므로 doesn't[does not] stop이 알맞다.

16 '~하고 있었다'는 과거진행형을 써서 「be동사의 과거형 + 동사원형-ing」 형태로 나타낸다. 주어가 복수(The girls)이므로 be동사는 were가 알맞다.

17 과거(yesterday)의 일을 묻고 있다. 일반동사 과거형의 의문문은 「Did + 주어 + 동사원형?」 형태이다.

CHAPTER
02

Present Perfect
현재완료

UNIT 03 현재완료 1
Present Perfect 1

LET'S CHECK
p.31, 33

A

1 과거시제 2 현재완료 3 현재완료
4 과거시제 5 현재완료 6 과거시제
7 과거시제 8 현재완료

B

1 Has Emma found her book?
2 I haven't[have not] driven a car before.
3 Have you seen my bag?
4 Have they gone to Spain?

C

1 ate, eaten 2 gave, given 3 fell, fallen
4 took, taken 5 drove, driven
6 rode, ridden 7 hid, hidden
8 broke, broken 9 spoke, spoken
10 got, gotten 11 wore, worn
12 grew, grown 13 threw, thrown
14 drank, drunk 15 sang, sung
16 swam, swum 17 went, gone
18 had, had 19 made, made
20 built, built 21 sent, sent 22 left, left
23 lost, lost 24 slept, slept 25 felt, felt
26 met, met 27 sat, sat 28 won, won
29 sold, sold 30 heard, heard
31 found, found 32 bought, bought
33 caught, caught 34 taught, taught
35 came, come 36 ran, run 37 cut, cut
38 hit, hit 39 read, read

LET'S PRACTICE
p.34-35

A

1 come 2 run 3 eaten 4 fallen 5 been
6 known 7 given 8 seen 9 written

B

1 has broken
2 hasn't[has not] left
3 have opened

C

1 Has, missed / hasn't 2 Has, made / has
3 Has, bought / hasn't
4 Have, washed / have

D

1 met 2 has 3 hasn't 4 hasn't
5 have not watched 6 Have 7 read
8 lost

UNIT 04 현재완료 2
Present Perfect 2

LET'S CHECK
p.37, 39

A

1 경험 2 완료 3 계속 4 경험 5 계속
6 경험 7 결과 8 계속 9 결과

B

1 for 2 since 3 for 4 for 5 since
6 since 7 for 8 for 9 since

C

1 have lived 2 have read 3 Did you watch
4 has Mr. Smith taught 5 left
6 did you finish 7 have been 8 landed

D

1 (1) have lived (2) lived
2 (1) has been (2) was
3 (1) have eaten (2) ate
4 (1) hasn't[has not] read (2) didn't[did not] read

LET'S PRACTICE
p.40-41

A

1 already 2 yet 3 never 4 for 5 since

B

1 slept 2 met 3 eaten 4 told
5 forgotten

C

1 has gone 2 has had 3 have watched
4 has lost

D

1 lived   **2** have never eaten   **3** has had
4 since   **5** Have they   **6** have you had
7 met   **8** didn't sleep

LET'S WRITE

p.42-43

STEP 1

1 has worked   **2** has, finished
3 Have you, been   **4** has gone
5 haven't, read

STEP 2

6 We have known each other for five years.
7 Steve has just opened the file.
8 Have you ever eaten Thai food?
9 I have never seen her before.
10 Somebody has taken my bag.

STEP 3

11 They have just left the station.
12 We have already sold the sofa.
13 Tim hasn't[has not] cleaned his room yet.
14 I have been here before.
15 He has never traveled abroad.
16 We have eaten at the restaurant many times.
17 Chris has broken his leg.
18 My mom has passed her driving test.
19 He has driven a car since 2014.
20 We have been good friends for 10 years.

REVIEW TEST

p.44-45

1 ④   **2** ⑤   **3** ③   **4** ⑤   **5** has lost
6 have lived   **7** ④   **8** ④   **9** ④   **10** ③
11 ⑤   **12** ④   **13** has visited → visited
14 didn't → haven't
15 have already heard
16 have known   **17** has never been

해설

1 ④ come의 과거분사형은 come이다. (come – came – come)

2 have/has 뒤에는 과거분사형이 온다. 따라서 ⑤ written이 알맞다.

3 missed 앞에 올 수 있는 조동사는 have/has이며, 주

어가 Tom이므로 ③ Has가 알맞다. ①④ be동사 뒤에는 일반동사가 올 수 없으며, ② Did 뒤에는 동사원형이 온다.

4 현재완료 뒤에 「since + 과거 시점」이 나오면 '~부터 계속 …하다'의 의미이다. ③ for 뒤에는 기간을 나타내는 말이 온다.

5 과거에 일어난 일의 결과가 현재까지 영향을 미치는 상태는 현재완료로 나타낸다. 주어가 3인칭 단수(Eric)이므로 has lost가 알맞다. (Eric은 그의 우산을 잃어버린 상태이다.)

6 과거부터 현재까지 계속되는 일은 현재완료로 나타낸다. 주어가 I이므로 have lived가 알맞다. (나는 여기에 5년째 살고 있다.)

7 「Have you ever + 과거분사?」(~해 본 적이 있니?)는 경험을 나타낸다. ①② 완료 ③ 결과 ④ 경험 ⑤ 계속

8 '~에 가 본 적이 있다'는 have/has been to로 나타낸다. (cf. have gone to: ~에 가고 (지금 여기에) 없다)

9 「since + 과거 시점」은 현재완료, two days ago는 과거시제와 어울리는 표현이다.

10 「How long + 현재완료?」는 '~한지 얼마나 되었니?'의 의미로 기간에 대해 묻는 말이다.

11 ① have → has rained, ② has wash → has washed, ③ haven't never met → haven't met 또는 have never met, ④ has become → became으로 고쳐야 알맞다.

12 과거 특정 시점을 나타내는 말이 올 경우에는 과거시제를 쓴다. ① When has the game started? → When did the game start?, ② have seen → saw, ③ has been sick → was sick, ④ has lived → lived로 고쳐야 알맞다.

13 in 2017은 과거 특정 시점을 나타내므로 has visited → visited로 고쳐야 알맞다.

14 yet(아직)은 현재완료와 어울리는 표현이다. 주어가 They이므로 didn't → haven't로 고쳐야 알맞다.

15 already(이미)는 현재완료와 함께 쓰여 어떤 일이 이미 완료된 상태임을 나타낸다. 주어가 We이므로 have already heard가 알맞다.

16 과거부터 현재까지 계속되는 일은 현재완료로 나타낸다. 주어가 I이므로 have known이 알맞다.

17 '~한 적이 있다[없다]'라고 경험에 대해 말할 때는 현재완료로 나타낸다. 주어가 3인칭 단수(Jiho)이므로 has never been이 알맞다.

CHAPTER
03

To-Infinitives, Gerunds
To부정사, 동명사

UNIT 05 To부정사
To-Infinitives

LET'S CHECK

p.49, 51

A

1 ⓑ   2 ⓑ   3 ⓒ   4 ⓑ   5 ⓒ   6 ⓐ   7 ⓐ

B

1 go   2 be   3 To give   4 eat   5 join
6 to watch   7 to speak   8 stay   9 wear

C

1 The dog is looking for something to eat.
2 He is not a man to tell a lie.
3 I want a book to read.
4 Do you have some money to buy snacks?
5 It's your turn to cook dinner.
6 I have a question to ask you.
7 It is time to say goodbye.
8 Susie has a lot of friends to help her.
9 We have some water to drink.

D

1 to write an email   2 to return the books
3 to read my card   4 to hear the noise
5 to win a gold medal

LET'S PRACTICE

p.52-53

A

1 명사   2 형용사   3 형용사   4 부사
5 형용사   6 명사   7 부사   8 부사

B

1 I'm busy. I have a lot of work do
2 I am glad see you again.
3 Do you want go to the beach?
4 Be a parent is not easy.
5 See is believe
6 She hopes be a teacher.

7 We are going out eat dinner.
8 It is dangerous play with fire.
9 I'm so tired. I don't have enough time sleep.

C

1 to read   2 to catch   3 to see

D

1 wanted to eat   2 is to have
3 many things to do   4 to buy a present
5 happy to help

UNIT 06 동명사
Gerunds

LET'S CHECK

p.55, 57

A

1 Watching   2 Buying   3 Eating
4 cooking   5 playing   6 reading
7 coming   8 being   9 learning   10 fixing
11 driving   12 listening   13 making
14 teaching

B

1 to quit   2 eating, to eat
3 moving, to move   4 cooking   5 waiting
6 smoking   7 talking   8 to pass
9 eating, to eat   10 snowing, to snow
11 watching, to watch   12 to leave
13 to help   14 reading   15 to go
16 memorizing   17 studying, to study
18 playing   19 going   20 answering
21 going   22 to live

LET'S PRACTICE

p.58-59

A

1 ⓑ   2 ⓒ   3 ⓐ   4 ⓑ   5 ⓒ   6 ⓐ   7 ⓑ

B

1 designing   2 listening   3 moving
4 speaking

C

1 doing her homework   2 opening the door
3 to go to the dentist

D

1 fishing   2 to take   3 to be   4 trying
5 going   6 watching   7 telling   8 driving

9 to build

LET'S WRITE
p.60-61

STEP 1

1 to watch 2 to be 3 to show 4 to go
5 writing

STEP 2

6 Driving at night is dangerous.
7 His job is to study birds.
8 Leaves began to fall.
9 I have homework to do
10 People shake hands to say hello.

STEP 3

11 I want to get good grades.
12 He promised to keep the secret.
13 John decided to marry her.
14 I love walking[to walk] in the forest.
15 I enjoy watching movies in my free time.
16 She practices speaking English every day.
17 They kept walking.
18 He bought some books to read.
19 We got up early to see the sunrise.
20 Tom was happy to score a goal.

REVIEW TEST
p.62-63

1 ③ 2 ④ 3 ③ 4 ④ 5 ② 6 ①
7 ④ 8 ④ 9 ⑤ 10 ⑤ 11 ② 12 ③
13 going → go 14 read → reading
15 Climbing the mountain is difficult.
16 He didn't have money to buy food.
17 to buy a new bike

해설

1 동사가 문장에서 명사처럼 주어로 쓰일 때는 동명사(또는 to부정사) 형태가 되어야 한다.

2 감정을 나타내는 형용사 뒤에 to부정사가 쓰이면 '~해서, ~하니'의 의미로 감정의 원인을 나타낸다.

3 전치사(at) 뒤에 동사가 올 때는 동명사 형태로 써야 한다.

4 enjoy는 목적어로 동명사를 쓴다.

5 동사가 문장에서 명사처럼 주격 보어로 쓰일 때는 동명사 또는 to부정사 형태가 되어야 한다. ② teach는 동사원형이므로 올 수 없다.

6 주어로 쓰인 to부정사구(To learn a new language)는 가주어 It으로 대신하고 문장 뒤로 보낼 수 있다.

7 ①②③⑤는 to부정사가 형용사처럼 쓰여 앞의 명사를 꾸며주고 있다. ④는 부사처럼 쓰여 '~하기 위해'라는 목적의 뜻을 나타낸다.

8 ①②③⑤는 동사가 문장에서 명사처럼 주어, 목적어, 주격 보어로 쓰여 '~하는 것'이란 뜻을 나타내므로 동명사이다. ④는 현재진행형으로 쓰여 '~하고 있다, ~하는 중이다'란 뜻을 나타낸다.

9 동사 promise는 목적어로 to부정사를 쓰고, mind는 목적어로 동명사를 쓴다.

10 ⑤ 동사 need는 목적어로 to부정사만을 쓸 수 있다.

11 ② 동사 decide는 목적어로 to부정사를 쓴다. 따라서 buying → buy로 고쳐야 알맞다.

12 ①②④⑤는 뒤의 to부정사구(진주어)를 대신하므로 가주어 It이다. ③의 It은 '그것'이라는 뜻의 대명사이며, 뒤의 to solve는 진주어가 아니라 명사 question을 꾸며주므로 형용사처럼 쓰인 to부정사이다.

13 동사 need는 목적어로 to부정사를 쓴다. to부정사는 「to + 동사원형」 형태이므로 going → go로 고쳐야 알맞다.

14 동사 finish는 목적어로 동명사를 쓴다. 따라서 read → reading으로 고쳐야 알맞다.

15 주어 '그 산을 등반하는 것'은 Climbing the mountain으로 나타낼 수 있다.

16 '음식을 살 돈'은 money to buy로 나타낼 수 있다.

17 '새 자전거를 사기 위해'는 to buy a new bike로 나타낼 수 있다.

CHAPTER
04

Various Verbs
여러 가지 동사

UNIT 07 여러 가지 동사 1
Various Verbs 1

LET'S CHECK
p.67

A

1 salty 2 good 3 soft 4 busy
5 sounds 6 tastes 7 smells
8 smells like 9 looks like

B

1 Regular exercise keeps you healthy.
2 Linda found the math test difficult.
3 The bad food made the boy sick.
4 My grandma calls me Sweetie.
5 They named their daughter Julie.
6 We elected Dave the captain of our team.
7 Jennifer found the movie boring.
8 The cook made the soup spicy.
9 He made his youngest son the king.

LET'S PRACTICE

p.68-69

A

1 (1) looks (2) sounds
2 (1) smells (2) taste
3 (1) smells (2) feels

B

1 looks expensive
2 taste fantastic
3 sounds beautiful

C

1 found 2 named 3 keep 4 called
5 easy 6 bright 7 your best friend
8 him their leader
9 the TV program useful

D

1 The song made her famous.
2 Natasha keeps her kitchen clean.
3 His friends call him a genius.
4 The town elected Mr. Brown mayor.

UNIT 08 여러 가지 동사 2
Various Verbs 2

LET'S CHECK

p.71

A

1 My grandmother gave me some money.
2 Amy will buy her mom a present.
3 Tony made his parents breakfast.
4 Elli sent her friends Christmas cards.
5 I lent George my baseball glove.
6 Can you bring me some water?
7 Jake told us a funny story.
8 The man asked me my name.
9 Janet taught the children a song.

B

1 to 2 to 3 to 4 to 5 to 6 to 7 for
8 for 9 of

LET'S PRACTICE

p.72-73

A

1 O 2 X 3 X 4 X 5 O 6 O 7 X
8 X 9 O

B

1 made me pizza
2 showed Jane his room
3 asked me the way to the station

C

1 to 2 for 3 of 4 for 5 me your pen
6 my cousin a postcard 7 the ball to me
8 the news to everyone 9 the menu for me

D

1 his new camera to me
2 dinner for us
3 yoga to her students
4 invitations to her friends

LET'S WRITE

p.74-75

STEP 1

1 felt 2 tastes 3 made 4 call
5 showed

STEP 2

6 The story sounds strange.
7 This seatbelt will keep you safe.
8 We elected Jack class president.
9 She didn't tell me anything.
10 Mom made cookies for my friends.

STEP 3

11 The man looks perfect.
12 This shampoo smells sweet.
13 That sounds like an interesting idea.

14 The campfire kept us warm.

15 She found the final exam difficult.

16 I named my bike Fred.

17 Books give us a lot of information.

18 The waiter brought me a glass of water.

19 Jackie teaches music to students.

20 He asked some questions of me.

REVIEW TEST

p.76-77

1 ②　2 ⑤　3 ②　4 ③　5 ⑤

6 Mr. Lee teaches us science.

7 She found the boy honest.

8 The school elected him student of the year.

9 ②　10 ②　11 ⑤　12 ⑤

13 softly → soft　14 for → to

15 taste sour　16 lent my notebook to him

17 made her unhappy

해설

1 감각동사 feel, look, taste, smell, sound 뒤에는 형용사가 주격 보어로 쓰인다. ② well은 부사이므로 good으로 고쳐야 알맞다.

2 give, send, show, pass는 모두 수여동사로 「동사 + 간접목적어 + 직접목적어」 또는 「동사 + 직접목적어 + to + 간접목적어」 형태로 쓸 수 있다. buy는 간접목적어가 직접목적어 뒤에 올 경우 전치사 for를 쓴다.

3 '~을 …하게 만들다'는 「make + 목적어 + 목적격 보어(형용사)」로 나타낸다. ② sadly → sad

4 감각동사 뒤에 명사가 올 경우에는 전치사 like(~처럼)를 쓴다. ③ smells chicken → smells like chicken

5 '~에게 …을 만들어주다'는 「make + 간접목적어 + 직접목적어」 또는 「make + 직접목적어 + for + 간접목적어」로 나타낸다.

6 '~에게 …을 가르쳐주다'는 「teach + 간접목적어 + 직접목적어」 또는 「teach + 직접목적어 + to + 간접목적어」로 나타낸다.

7 '~가 …인 것을 알게 되다, ~가 …라고 생각하다'는 「found + 목적어 + 목적격 보어(형용사)」로 나타낸다.

8 '~을 …로 선출하다'는 「elect + 목적어 + 목적격 보어(명사)」로 나타낸다.

9 '~하게 보이다'는 「look + 형용사」, '~가 …라는 것을 알게 되다'는 「find + 목적어 + 목적격 보어(형용사)」로 나타낸다.

10 '~에게 …을 묻다'는 「ask + 간접목적어 + 직접목적어」 또는 「ask + 직접목적어 + of + 간접목적어」 형

태로 나타낸다.

11 ①②③④는 「동사 + 목적어 + 목적격 보어」, ⑤는 「동사 + 간접목적어 + 직접목적어」 형태의 문장이다.

12 ①②③④는 「동사 + 간접목적어 + 직접목적어」, ⑤는 「동사 + 목적어 + 목적격 보어」 형태의 문장이다.

13 감각동사 feel 뒤에는 형용사가 주격 보어로 쓰인다. softly는 부사이므로 soft로 고쳐야 알맞다.

14 '~에게 …을 쓰다'는 「write + 간접목적어 + 직접목적어」 또는 「write + 직접목적어 + to + 간접목적어」로 나타낸다. 따라서 for를 to로 고쳐야 알맞다.

15 '~한 맛이 나다'는 「taste + 형용사」로 나타낸다.

16 '~에게 …을 빌려주다'는 「lend + 간접목적어 + 직접목적어」 또는 「lend + 직접목적어 + to + 간접목적어」로 나타낸다.

17 '~을 …하게 만들다'는 「make + 목적어 + 목적격 보어(형용사)」로 나타낸다.

CHAPTER 05

The Passive
수동태

UNIT 09 수동태 1
The Passive 1

LET'S CHECK

p.81

A

1 steal　2 be invited　3 make　4 be helped
5 deliver　6 be grown　7 read　8 be sold
9 be broken

B

1 (1) made　(2) was made
2 (1) was created　(2) created
3 (1) stole　(2) was stolen
4 (1) is spoken　(2) speak

LET'S PRACTICE

p.82-83

A

1 수동태　2 능동태　3 수동태　4 수동태
5 수동태　6 능동태　7 수동태　8 능동태

B

1 read　2 hid　3 was bitten　4 took
5 cleans　6 was found　7 was waken
8 wasn't written　9 don't grow

C

1 chased　2 planted　3 was canceled

D

1 This hotel was built
2 The fish was caught
3 My bike was stolen
4 Shoes are not made

UNIT 10 수동태 2
The Passive 2

LET'S CHECK

p.85

A

1 are used　2 is loved　3 is taught
4 are sold

B

1 was played　2 was painted
3 were destroyed　4 was written

LET'S PRACTICE

p.86-87

A

1 is served　2 are parked　3 are washed

B

1 were built　2 are cut　3 was painted
4 is spoken　5 was hit　6 was invented
7 was found　8 is walked　9 were sent

C

1 The shop is closed by the manager.
2 The flat tire was changed by Robert.
3 The accident was seen by many people.
4 The mistakes were corrected by the teacher.

D

1 invited　2 enjoyed　3 was stolen
4 grow　5 broke　6 was eaten

7 designed　8 by him　9 wasn't paid

LET'S WRITE

p.88-89

STEP 1

1 was stolen　2 is used　3 are sold
4 was built　5 were parked

STEP 2

6 Sam was stung by a bee.
7 This email was written by Kevin.
8 Cotton candy is made of sugar.
9 The book was published in 1997.
10 The actor is loved by many people.

STEP 3

11 Cricket is played in England.
12 Frogs are eaten by snakes.
13 The lock was broken by someone.
14 The building was designed by an Italian.
15 English and French are spoken in Canada.
16 We were invited to Helen's wedding.
17 The bottles are placed on the shelf.
18 A hundred people were killed in the plane crash.
19 My computer was delivered on Monday.
20 The roses were planted by my grandmother.

REVIEW TEST

p.90-91

1 ③　2 ④　3 ⑤　4 ⑤　5 ④
6 The magazine is read by many women.
7 ⑤　8 ④　9 ④　10 ③　11 ②
12 is grown　13 was fixed　14 is spoken
15 was worn　16 were eaten

해설

1 '차려졌다'는 수동태(be + 과거분사)를 사용하여 ③ was set으로 나타낼 수 있다.

2 수동태 문장에서 행위자는 「by + 목적격」으로 나타낸다. ④ they는 주격 대명사이므로 알맞지 않다.

3 This picture가 주어인 경우 행동의 대상이므로 수동태가 적절하다. 과거시제의 수동태는 「was/were + 과거분사」의 형태이므로 ⑤가 알맞다.

4 주어(She)가 행동의 대상이므로 수동태가 적절하다. 과거시제 수동태의 부정형은 「wasn't/weren't + 과거분사」의 형태이므로 ⑤가 알맞다.

5 수동태 문장에서 행위자가 일반적인 사람들이거나 중요하지 않은 경우 「by + 목적격」은 생략할 수 있다. 그러나 ④의 Mr. Kim은 특정인을 가리키므로 생략할 수 없다.

6 수동태는 주어 뒤에 「be동사 + 과거분사」가 오고, 그 뒤에 행위자를 「by + 목적격」으로 나타낸다.

7 ⑤ The man이 행위자이므로 능동태가 적절하다. (was stolen → stole)

8 ④ The game은 시청되는 것이므로 수동태가 적절하다 (watched → was watched)

9 ① finish → was finished, ② was enjoyed → enjoyed, ③ bought → was bought, ⑤ was made → made로 고쳐야 알맞다.

10 Emma는 행위자이므로 did, The laundry는 행동의 대상이므로 「be동사 + 과거분사」 형태인 was done이 알맞다.

11 ② 과거시제의 수동태는 「was/were + 과거분사」의 형태이므로 were made로 써야 알맞다.

12 주어 Coffee가 단수이고 현재시제이므로 is grown이 알맞다.

13 주어 The door가 단수이고 과거시제이므로 was fixed가 알맞다.

14 주어 Dutch가 단수이고 현재시제이므로 is spoken이 알맞다.

15 주어 This wedding dress가 단수이고 과거시제이므로 was worn이 알맞다.

16 주어 The cookies가 복수이고 과거시제이므로 were eaten이 알맞다.

CHAPTER
06

Conjunctions
접속사

접속사 1
UNIT 11
Conjunctions 1

LET'S CHECK p.95

A
1 but 2 or 3 but 4 and 5 but 6 or
7 so 8 but 9 and

B
1 ⓑ 2 ⓐ 3 ⓖ 4 ⓔ 5 ⓒ 6 ⓓ

LET'S PRACTICE p.96-97

A
1 so 2 but 3 or 4 and 5 but 6 or
7 so 8 and 9 or

B
1 or 2 so 3 but

C
1 Is that a duck or a goose?
2 The ship carries people and things.
3 Tom did his best but failed the exam.
4 It was dusty outside, so I closed the window.

D
1 or 2 so 3 and 4 or 5 so 6 but
7 but 8 so 9 or

접속사 2
UNIT 12
Conjunctions 2

LET'S CHECK p.99

A
1 while 2 after 3 because 4 If
5 Before

B
1 ⓒ 2 ⓖ 3 ⓐ 4 ⓕ 5 ⓑ 6 ⓓ

LET'S PRACTICE p.100-101

A
1 I'll make a snowman
2 when I found him
3 while you are driving
4 because it was sunny

B
1 while 2 because 3 If 4 when 5 after
6 before 7 while 8 are 9 don't

C

1 If 2 before 3 because

D

1 You can use my phone, you need it
2 Peter fell asleep, he was reading
3 I drank a glass of water, I was thirsty
4 You will catch the bus, you run

LET'S WRITE

p.102-103

STEP 1

1 and 2 or 3 when 4 because 5 If

STEP 2

6 Sally can sing and dance.
7 She is young but wise.
8 ate dinner after Dad came home
9 Will you have coffee or tea?
10 go home before it gets dark

STEP 3

11 and moved to New York
12 but it wasn't[was not] cold
13 a knife or scissors
14 When the phone rang
15 While I am studying
16 before he came in
17 After he woke up
18 if you study hard
19 so he can speak English well
20 Because we are friends

REVIEW TEST

p.104-105

1 ④ 2 ⑤ 3 ④ 4 ① 5 because
6 When 7 Before 8 ④ 9 ② 10 ③
11 ④ 12 ③ 13 Because 14 but
15 interesting and useful
16 while they are eating 17 If it rains

해설

1 서로 비슷한 내용은 ④ and로 연결한다.
2 '나는 그 영화가 너무 폭력적이기 때문에 좋아하지 않는다'고 해야 자연스럽다. ⑤ because
3 '그가 집에 왔을 때 저녁 식사가 준비되어 있었다'고 해야 자연스럽다. ④ when
4 '우리는 내일 날씨가 맑으면 동물원에 갈 것이다'라고

해야 자연스럽다. ① if
5 두 문장 모두 뒷 문장이 앞 문장의 이유를 설명하고 있으므로 because가 알맞다.
6 '13살의 나이에'는 '그가 13살이었을 때'라는 절로 바꿀 수 있다.
7 'TV를 끄고 방을 나갔다'는 '방을 나가기 전에 TV를 껐다'로 바꿀 수 있다.
8 ①②③⑤는 서로 비슷한 내용을 연결하므로 and, ④는 선택해야 할 것을 연결하므로 or이 알맞다.
9 시간과 조건의 부사절에서는 미래형 대신 현재형을 쓴다. ② will work → work
10 서로 비슷한 내용은 and, 선택해야 할 것은 or로 연결한다.
11 '우리는 가격이 쌌기 때문에 버스로 갔다', '네가 일찍 온다면 자리를 잡을 수 있다'라고 해야 자연스럽다.
12 ①②④⑤는 접속사, ③은 의문사이다.
13 '～때문에'는 Because가 적절하다.
14 '하지만, 그러나'는 but이 적절하다.
15 서로 비슷한 내용은 and로 연결한다.
16 '～하는 동안'은 while을 사용한다.
17 '(만약) ～한다면'은 if를 사용한다.

CHAPTER 07

Relative Pronouns
관계대명사

UNIT 13 관계대명사 1
Relative Pronouns 1

LET'S CHECK

p.109

A

1 A thief is a person who steals things.
2 He lives in a house that has a pool.
3 I ate the noodles which my mom made.
4 John is the boy who is riding the bike.
5 This is the movie that I watched last night.

6 The patient pointed at the tooth that hurt.
7 Terry is wearing socks which have holes.
8 Is there a shop which sells fruit?
9 Is that the policeman who helped you?

B

1 (1) ⓑ (2) ⓐ   2 (1) ⓐ (2) ⓑ
3 (1) ⓑ (2) ⓐ   4 (1) ⓐ (2) ⓑ

C

1 who   2 who   3 which   4 which   5 who
6 who   7 which   8 who   9 which

D

1 are   2 lives   3 study   4 were   5 makes
6 is   7 sells   8 opens   9 are

LET'S PRACTICE
p.110-111

A

1 which   2 who   3 who   4 which   5 who
6 which   7 which   8 who   9 which

B

1 ⓒ   2 ⓑ   3 ⓐ   4 ⓐ

C

1 which washes dirty dishes
2 who treats sick animals
3 which cleans floors automatically

D

1 which lives in the desert
2 which didn't fit him well
3 who called me
4 which is near the hotel

UNIT 14 관계대명사 2
Relative Pronouns 2

LET'S CHECK
p.115

A

1 주격   2 주격   3 목적격   4 주격   5 목적격
6 목적격   7 주격

B

1 The actor we met is not famous.
2 These are shoes I usually wear.
3 Brian is a person everybody likes.
4 The man we took this morning was empty.
5 The dress you're wearing is nice.

6 The boy I called didn't answer the phone.
7 All the guests Amy invited came to the party.
8 I liked the museum we visited last weekend.
9 My mom liked my friend I brought home
   yesterday.

LET'S PRACTICE
p.116-117

A

1 ⓒ, ⓓ   2 ⓐ, ⓑ, ⓓ   3 ⓒ, ⓓ   4 ⓒ, ⓓ

B

1 X   2 O   3 X   4 X   5 O   6 X   7 O
8 X   9 O

C

1 which we made
2 which I set last night
3 who(m) he likes

D

1 which you are wearing
2 who(m) she met at her university
3 which I borrowed from my friend
4 who(m) Jamie teaches

LET'S WRITE
p.118-119

STEP 1

1 which   2 which   3 who   4 whom
5 who

STEP 2

6 who wrote this book
7 which can sing and dance
8 which Carol made
9 who is taller than him
10 which we took yesterday

STEP 3

11 who love animals
12 (which[that]) we watched yesterday
13 (who(m)[that]) Tom likes
14 (which[that]) I wrote
15 which[that] has a lot of beautiful beaches
16 (which[that]) I recommended
17 who[that] lives next door
18 which[that] were in the refrigerator
19 (which[that]) I bought on the Internet
20 who[that] wants to be a ballerina

p.120-121

1 ②　2 who　3 which　4 whom　5 ②
6 ④　7 ⑤　8 ③　9 ②　10 ②　11 ③
12 ③
13 I like the soup which my mom makes.
14 The computer which he wants to buy
15 which[that] my parents grow
16 who[that] stole my money

해설

1 첫 번째 문장은 선행사 a friend가 사람이고 형용사절 에서 동사 lives의 주어 역할을 하므로 주격 관계대명사 who[that]가 알맞다. 두 번째 문장은 선행사 the book이 사물이고 형용사절에서 동사 lost의 목적어 역할을 하므로 목적격 관계대명사 which[that]가 알맞다.

2 선행사 The man이 사람이고 형용사절에서 동사 invited의 주어 역할을 하므로 주격 관계대명사 who가 알맞다.

3 선행사 The opera가 사물이고 형용사절에서 동사 watched의 목적어 역할을 하므로 목적격 관계대명사 which[that]가 알맞다.

4 선행사 the girl이 사람이고 형용사절에서 전치사 to의 목적어 역할을 하므로 목적격 관계대명사 whom[that]이 알맞다.

5 선행사 The buses가 사물이므로 관계대명사는 which, that을 쓰고, 관계대명사 뒤의 동사는 선행사의 수에 일치시켜야 하므로 go가 알맞다. run이 문장 전체의 동사이므로 ①은 알맞지 않다.

6 관계대명사 which는 선행사가 사물, 동물일 때 쓴다.

7 목적격 관계대명사 뒤에는 「주어＋동사」 형태가, 주격 관계대명사 뒤에는 동사가 이어진다. ①②③④는 주격, ⑤는 목적격 관계대명사이다.

8 ①②④⑤는 목적격 관계대명사로 생략할 수 있으나,③은 주격 관계대명사로 생략할 수 없다.

9 Peter sent me yesterday는 선행사 the email을 꾸며주는 형용사절이며, 앞에 목적격 관계대명사 which 또는 that이 생략되어 있다.

10 관계대명사 that은 선행사의 종류에 관계없이 모두 쓸 수 있다.

11 ③ 선행사 a friend가 사람이므로 사물, 동물을 나타내는 관계대명사 which 대신 who 또는 that을 써야 알맞다.

12 ③ 관계대명사 뒤에 동사(lived)가 이어지므로 whom 대신 주격 관계대명사 who[that]를 써야 알맞다.

13 관계대명사 which가 형용사절에서 동사 makes의 목적어 역할을 하므로 목적어 it을 중복으로 쓰지 않는다.

14 '그가 사고 싶은 컴퓨터'이므로 The computer가 선행사가 되고 그 뒤에 「목적격 관계대명사＋주어＋동사」의 어순을 따른다.

15 선행사 the vegetables가 사물이므로 관계대명사 which 또는 that을 써서 형용사절을 만든다.

16 선행사 the man이 사람이므로 관계대명사 who 또는 that을 써서 형용사절을 만든다.

WORKBOOK

UNIT 01 현재시제, 현재진행형
Present Simple, Present Continuous

p.4-5

A
1 is　2 get　3 cries　4 speaks　5 play
6 isn't[is not]　7 don't[do not] go　8 Are
9 Do, eat

B
1 are falling　2 is taking　3 are crossing
4 is cutting　5 are lying　6 isn't writing
7 aren't flying　8 Is, reading　9 Are, waiting

C
1 know　2 is eating　3 hugs　4 has
5 is wearing　6 aren't studying
7 once a month　8 Do you want
9 Does she go

D
1 is cutting　2 Is she writing
3 doesn't[does not] drink　4 Do you wear

UNIT 02 과거시제, 과거진행형
Past Simple, Past Continuous

p.6-7

A

1 are 2 was 3 were 4 ate 5 go
6 worked 7 helped 8 didn't speak
9 Did they enjoy

B

1 are watching 2 were sleeping
3 was raining 4 is drawing 5 is getting
6 aren't[are not] studying
7 weren't[were not] studying 8 Is, going
9 were, doing

C

1 Did / did 2 Were / weren't 3 Did / didn't
4 Were / were

D

1 was running 2 didn't work
3 Did you have 4 Were they playing

UNIT 03 현재완료 1
Present Perfect 1

p.8-9

A

1 visited, visited 2 did, done 3 ate, eaten
4 wrote, written 5 met, met
6 bought, bought 7 came, come
8 ran, run 9 cut, cut

B

1 have arrived 2 hasn't[has not] sold
3 have gone 4 has lost
5 haven't[have not] read 6 has worked
7 has been 8 has broken
9 haven't[have not] finished

C

1 Have, seen / haven't
2 Has, left / has
3 Have, studied / have
4 Have, heard / haven't

D

1 Has, stopped 2 hasn't[has not] answered
3 has traveled 4 Have, found

UNIT 04 현재완료 2
Present Perfect 2

p.10-11

A

1 hasn't[has not] finished 2 have, cleaned
3 Have, seen 4 has, eaten 5 have climbed
6 has had 7 has been 8 has gone
9 has lost

B

1 was 2 has been 3 haven't 4 rode
5 Have / have 6 left 7 have you had
8 has driven 9 done / have

C

1 ago 2 yet 3 for 4 last night 5 since

D

1 Have you ever seen
2 hasn't[has not] come
3 has just landed
4 have never played

UNIT 05 To부정사
To-Infinitives

p.12-13

A

1 ⓑ 2 ⓐ 3 ⓐ 4 ⓑ 5 ⓐ 6 ⓒ 7 ⓐ
8 ⓒ 9 ⓑ

B

1 There are lots of things to see in New York.
2 The boy has no friends to play with.
3 What is the best way to get to the station?
4 Karen always takes a book to read.
5 Do you want something to drink?
6 It is time to go home.
7 She has three puppies to take care of.

C

1 ⓖ 2 ⓓ 3 ⓑ 4 ⓗ 5 ⓒ 6 ⓐ 7 ⓕ

D

1 to swim   2 It, to watch   3 to learn

4 happy to get

_{UNIT}06 동명사
Gerunds

p.14-15

A

1 ⓐ   2 ⓒ   3 ⓑ   4 ⓑ   5 ⓒ   6 ⓑ   7 ⓐ

8 ⓐ

B

1 to drive   2 to do   3 going   4 to be

5 dancing   6 working, to work

7 playing, to play   8 to study   9 cooking

C

1 skiing   2 traveling   3 to do   4 to go

D

1 Writing   2 Listening   3 swimming

4 playing

_{UNIT}07 여러 가지 동사 1
Various Verbs 1

p.16-17

A

1 smells   2 sounds   3 tastes   4 feels

5 sleepy   6 lovely   7 terrible   8 felt

9 feel like

B

1 kept me awake

2 call you Tom

3 kept the food warm

4 made her famous

5 found my computer broken

6 elected him their next leader

7 named his dog Teddy

8 keep the classroom clean

9 found her homework easy

C

1 great   2 cold   3 O   4 O   5 looks like

6 interesting   7 O   8 healthy   9 him

D

1 sounds friendly

2 makes the Earth hotter

3 keep the children quiet

4 calls me Peter

_{UNIT}08 여러 가지 동사 2
Various Verbs 2

p.18-19

A

1 ⓐ   2 ⓐ   3 ⓑ   4 ⓐ   5 ⓑ   6 ⓐ   7 ⓑ

8 ⓑ   9 ⓐ

B

1 bought us pizza

2 made his brother a paper airplane

3 gave me her address

4 passed me the ball

5 teaches us math

6 sent me an invitation

7 brought us some ice

C

1 for me   2 to me   3 for Susie   4 of you

D

1 gave me a book

2 made me a cup of cocoa

3 buy me a new cellphone

4 bring me the remote control

_{UNIT}09 수동태 1
The Passive 1

p.20-21

A

1 깼다   2 심어졌다   3 사용한다   4 만들어진다

5 배달한다   6 취소되었다   7 발명했다

8 지어졌다   9 불려진다.

B

1 was finished   2 was caught   3 saw

4 took   5 were invited   6 is taught

7 was destroyed   8 was stolen   9 found

C

1 This book is read by many people.

2 The letters were sent two days ago.

3 The little boy was bitten by a dog.

4 The shirt was ironed by Tim.

D

1 is washed   2 was fixed   3 was stolen

4 are sent

UNIT 10 수동태 2
The Passive 2

p.22-23

A

1 is produced   2 was hit   3 was painted

4 is played   5 are used   6 are cleaned

7 were invited

B

1 His money was stolen by someone.

2 Cars are repaired by the mechanic.

3 The door was closed by her.

4 The dress was worn by the actress.

C

1 The people elect the president.

2 We turned on the TV.

3 The hotel guests use the swimming pool.

4 The teacher erased the blackboard.

D

1 is kept   2 was cut   3 was bitten

4 wasn't[was not] invited

UNIT 11 접속사 1
Conjunctions 1

p.24-25

A

1 and   2 or   3 and   4 or   5 or   6 so

7 but   8 but   9 so

B

1 or   2 and   3 but   4 so   5 or   6 but

7 so

C

1 She can play the piano and the guitar.

2 The line was long, so we waited for a long time.

3 Do you want to go with us or stay here?

4 He got a cold, but he didn't take any medicine.

D

1 so I called   2 but I bought

3 and made a snowman   4 now or later

UNIT 12 접속사 2
Conjunctions 2

p.26-27

A

1 when   2 while   3 after   4 before

5 before   6 when   7 if   8 when

9 because

B

1 because   2 after   3 while   4 If

5 before

C

1 While I was playing soccer, I hurt my ankle.

2 She felt sick after she ate the fish.

3 He called the police because he lost his wallet.

4 I will walk to school if the weather is good.

D

1 before he left   2 When I was young

3 after I finish   4 If Angela invites me

UNIT 13 관계대명사 1
Relative Pronouns 1

p.28-29

A

1 Cindy buys milk that is low fat.

2 I have an aunt who lives in Seattle.

3 Grace is the girl who is wearing the red dress.

4 The man who is in the kitchen is my father.

5 Tony is wearing (jeans) that are too tight.
6 (The cat) which scratched me is Sally's.
7 (The person) who sent the roses is Chris.
8 Amy bought (a bag) which cost $20.
9 Is there (a shop) which sells swimsuits?

B

1 who   2 which   3 that   4 which   5 who
6 who   7 which   8 who   9 who

C

1 I bought a dress which was on sale.
2 Do you see the cat which is on the roof?
3 The girl who came here was Karen.
4 She took out the ring which was in the box.

D

1 who served us
2 which keeps water warm
3 who can speak English
4 who saw the accident

UNIT 14 관계대명사 2
Relative Pronouns 2

p.30-31

A

1 목적격   2 주격   3 목적격   4 주격   5 주격
6 목적격   7 주격   8 목적격   9 주격

B

1 which   2 that   3 whom   4 that   5 that
6 whom   7 which   8 which   9 that

C

1 The cup which he dropped was broken.
2 She gave me the strawberry jam which she made.
3 The teacher who(m) I like the most is Mrs. Yoon.
4 This is the tree which my dad and I planted.

D

1 which my mom gave me
2 which he took
3 who(m) he likes
4 who(m) I meet

MEMO

MEMO

MEMO

MEMO

MEMO

MEMO